READING ABOUT SCIENCE
Skills and Concepts

John F. Mongillo
Ray Broekel
Beth S. Atwood
Donald L. Buchholz
Albert B. Carr
Claudia Cornett
Jacqueline L. Harris
Vivian Zwaik

Special Reading Consultant
Roger Farr
    Professor of Education
    Indiana University

D1258551

Phoenix Learning Resources
New York

E

PHOTO CREDITS

ISBN 0–7915–1205–3

(Previously ISBN 0–07–002425–1)

2 3 4 5 6 7 8 9 0 99 98 97 96 95 94 93

AUTHORS

John F. Mongillo
Editor in Chief, Science Department
Webster Division
McGraw-Hill Book Company
New York, New York

Dr. Ray Broekel
Author and Consultant
Ipswich, Massachusetts

Beth S. Atwood
Writer and Reading Consultant
Durham, Connecticut

Donald L. Buchholz
Developer of Curriculum Materials
Honolulu, Hawaii

Albert B. Carr
Professor of Science Education
University of Hawaii
Honolulu, Hawaii

Claudia Cornett
Assistant Professor of Education
Wittenberg University
Springfield, Ohio

Jacqueline L. Harris
Writer and Science Editor
Wethersfield, Connecticut

Vivian Zwaik
Writer and Educational Consultant
Glen Head, New York

Contributing Writers

Rita Harkins Dickinson
Special Education Instructor
Rio Salado Community College
Phoenix, Arizona

Myra J. Goldberg
Reading Consultant
Rye, New York

Adrienne Ballard Taylor
Junior High School Science Teacher
Black Mountain School
Cave Creek, Arizona

Bruce Tone
Editorial Associate
School of Education
Indiana University
Bloomington, Indiana

Dr. Clifford Watson
Staff Coordinator
Region 1
Detroit Public Schools
Detroit, Michigan

Reviewers

PRONUNCIATION GUIDE

Some words in this book may be unfamiliar to you and difficult for you to pronounce. These words are printed in italics. Then, they are spelled according to the way they are said, or pronounced. This phonetic spelling appears in parentheses next to the words. The pronunciation guide below will help you say the words.

ă	pat	î	dear, deer, fierce, mere	p	pop	zh	garage, pleasure; vision
ā	aid, fey, pay			r	roar	ə	about, silent pencil, lemon, circus
â	air, care, wear	j	judge	s	miss, sauce, see		
ä	father	k	cat, kick, pique	sh	dish, ship		
b	bib	l	lid, needle	t	tight	ər	butter
ch	church	m	am, man, mum	th	path, thin		
d	deed	n	no, sudden	*th*	bathe, this		
ĕ	pet, pleasure	ng	thing	ŭ	cut, rough		
ē	be, bee, easy, leisure	ŏ	horrible, pot	û	circle, firm, heard, term, turn, urge, word		
f	fast, fife, off, phase, rough	ō	go, hoarse, row, toe				STRESS
g	gag	ô	alter, caught, for, paw	v	cave, valve, vine		Primary stress '
h	hat	oi	boy, noise, oil	w	with		**bi·ol'o·gy**
hw	which	ou	cow, out	y	yes		[bī ŏl'ejē]
ĭ	pit	o͝o	took	yo͞o	abuse, use		Secondary stress'
ī	by, guy, pie	o͞o	boot, fruit	z	rose, size, xylophone, zebra		**bi'o·log'i·cal**
							[bī'elŏj'ĭkel]

The key to pronunciation above is reprinted by permission from *The American Heritage School Dictionary* copyright © 1977, by Houghton Mifflin Company.

TABLE OF CONTENTS

TO THE STUDENT

The world of science is a world of observing, exploring, predicting, reading, experimenting, testing, and recording. It is a world of trying and failing and trying again until, at last, you succeed. In the world of science, there is always some exciting discovery to be made and something new to explore.

In this book, you will learn about some of these explorations and discoveries. Through these readings about science, you will have a chance to join the crew of the *Alvin* and explore the strange world beneath the sea. You may hop aboard a hot-air balloon and float across the Atlantic Ocean or track cougars through the Rocky Mountains. You will learn that science is an important part of your life—and that reading about science is fun.

Three Areas of Science

READING ABOUT SCIENCE explores three areas of science: life science, earth-space science, and physical science. Each book in this series contains a unit on each of the three areas. Although there are different areas of science, it is important to remember that each area is related to the others in some way and that all areas are important to people.

Life science is the study of living things. Life scientists explore the world of plants, animals, and humans. Their goal is to find out how living things depend upon each other for survival and to observe how they live and interact in their environments, or surroundings.

The general area of life science includes many specialized areas, such as botany, zoology, and ecology. *Botanists* work mainly with plants. *Zoologists* work mostly with animals. *Ecologists* are scientists who study the effects of air pollution, water pollution, and noise pollution on living things.

Earth-space science is the study of our Earth and other bodies in the solar system. Some earth-space scientists are *meteorologists,* who study climate and weather; *geologists,* who study the earth, the way it was formed and its makeup, rocks and fossils, earthquakes, and volcanoes; *oceanographers,* who study currents, waves, and life in the oceans of the world; and *astronomers,* who study the solar system, including the sun and other stars, moons, and planets.

Physical science is the study of matter and energy. *Physicists* are physical scientists who explore topics such as matter, atoms, and nuclear energy. Other physical scientists study sound, magnetism, heat, light, electricity, water, and air. *Chemists* develop the substances used in medicine, clothing, food, and many other things.

All of these areas of science influence our everyday life. For example, our transportation and communications systems depend on the work of physical scientists. Together, physical scientists, earth-space scientists, and life scientists search for ways to solve problems and improve the quality of our everyday life.

In your reading, you may discover that there is one area of science that you like especially. The bibliography in the back of this book is divided into life, earth-space, and physical sciences. The books that are suggested will take you on more adventures in the world of science.

Reading Science Materials

Some students are nervous about taking courses in science. They think that science is too difficult, and so they give up even before they begin.

Think about this. Do you enjoy the world around you? Do you ever wonder why clouds have so many different shapes and what keeps planes up in the air? Did you ever want to explore a cave or find out why volcanoes erupt or why the earth shakes? If you can answer yes to any of those questions and if you are willing to read and think and investigate carefully the world around you, then you can do well in science and enjoy it, too!

Reading science materials is different from reading a magazine or a novel. You must take your time and think about what you are reading. Remember that science materials contain special vocabulary words. You will know some words. Other words may be familiar to you, but you may be unsure of their meanings. And still other words may be totally unfamiliar. It is these unfamiliar words in particular that make science reading seem difficult.

Steps to Follow

The suggestions that follow will help you use this book:

A.   Study the photo or drawing that goes with the story. Read the title and the sentences that are printed in blue. These are all clues to what the story is about.

B.   Study the words for the story in the list of Words to Know in the back of this book. You will find it easier to read the story if you understand the meanings of these words. Many times, you will find the meaning of the word right in the story.

When reading the story, look for clues to important words or ideas. Vocabulary words appear in a special print. Sometimes words or phrases are underlined. Pay special attention to these clues.

C.   Read the story carefully. Think about what you are reading. Are any of the ideas in the story things that you have heard or read about before?

D.   As you read, ask yourself questions. For example, "Why did the electricity go off?" "What caused the bears to turn green?" Many times, your questions are answered later in the story. Questioning helps you to understand what the author is saying. Asking questions also gets you ready for what comes next in the story.

E.   Pay special attention to diagrams, charts, and other visual aids. They will often help you to understand the story better.

F.   After you read the story slowly and carefully, you are ready to answer the questions on the Questions page. If the book you have is part of a classroom set, you should write your answers in a special notebook or on paper that you can keep in a folder. Do not write in this book without your teacher's permission.

Put your name, the title of the story, and its page number on a sheet of paper. Read each question carefully. Record the question number and your answer on your answer paper.

The questions in this book check for the following kinds of comprehension, or understanding:

1. *Science vocabulary comprehension.* This kind of question asks you to remember the meaning of a word or term used in the story.

2. *Literal comprehension.* This kind of question asks you to remember certain facts that are given in the story. For example, the story might state that a snake was over 5 meters long. A literal question would ask you: "How long was the snake?"

3. *Interpretive comprehension.* This kind of question asks you to think about the story. To answer the question, you must decide what the author means, not what is said, or stated, in the story. For example, you may be

asked what the *main idea* of the story is or what happened first, or what *caused* something to happen in the story.

4. *Applied comprehension.* This kind of question asks you to use what you have read to (1) solve a new problem, (2) interpret a chart or graph; or (3) put a certain topic under its correct heading, or category.

You should read each question carefully. You may go back to the story to help you find the answer. The questions are meant to help you learn how to read science better.

G. When you complete the Questions page, turn it in to your teacher. Or, with your teacher's permission, check your answers against the answer key in the *Teacher's Guide.* If you made a mistake, find out what you did wrong. Practice answering that kind of question, and you will do better the next time.

H. Turn to the directions that tell you how to keep your Progress Charts. If you are not supposed to write in this book, you may make a copy of each chart to keep in your READING ABOUT SCIENCE folder or notebook. You may be surprised to see how well you can read science.

Special Sections

There are some special sections that follow each of the three science units.

People to Know is about a person or a group of people who have done something special in the field of life science, earth-space science, or physical science. Some examples are Margaret Seddon, astronaut; Jacques Cousteau, undersea explorer; Benjamin Banneker, astronomer; and Mary Jean Currier, wildlife scientist.

Places to Go takes you on visits to aquariums, zoos, space centers, and museums all over the United States and in Canada.

Puzzles to Do includes crossword puzzles, hidden-word games, and mazes on many different topics in science.

Science Adventures gives you a chance to investigate interesting topics such as solar energy, making fossils, and extrasensory perception.

The last unit in the book is a special unit called Careers in Science. This unit gives you an opportunity to investigate hundreds of science-related careers.

You may decide to make science your lifelong hobby or even your career. Whatever you do, the authors of READING ABOUT SCIENCE hope that this book will help you discover the joys of science.

LIFE SCIENCE

People get messages about the world through their sense organs—the eyes, ears, nose, tongue, and skin. They "translate" those messages into action with the help of the body's nervous system. The sensory nerves carry messages, called nerve impulses, *to the brain. The brain sends back impulses through the motor nerves. These impulses cause muscles to move. What kinds of messages are these players giving to each other?*

Albinos Are Easy to See

Albinos are unusual-looking animals.

Linda and Carmen were on a hiking trip when suddenly they heard a hissing sound that spelled danger. They looked down at the rocks nearby and saw what had been making the noise. It was a snake. Linda and Carmen looked at the snake in astonishment. The girls had seen many snakes before, but never one like this. It was white and had pink eyes. They were looking at a rare albino snake.

An albino animal does not have enough *melanin* (mĕl'ə nĭn). Melanin is the chemical that gives animals their color. Pure albinos have no melanin at all in their bodies. Their eyes and ears are pink. And their skin, hair, or feathers are white. There are albino insects, fish, snakes, turtles, frogs, toads, and salamanders. There are also albino birds, mammals, and people. But among most kinds of animals, albinos are rare.

Most albino animals living in the wild do not have an easy time of it. Because of their light coloring, they do not blend in with their surroundings. This makes it easier for their enemies to see them. Albinos often have poor eyesight, so albino animals may have trouble finding food. Of all the kinds of albino animals, fish such as catfish do the best in the wild. That is because catfish are bottom feeders and do not need to use their eyes to find food.

1. A chemical that gives animals their color is called _____.

2. The snake described in the story is an _____.

3. Why did Linda and Carmen suddenly stop walking?
   a. They saw a snake in their path.
   b. They wanted to get a better look at the snake.
   c. They heard a sound that meant danger.

4. According to the story, albino catfish survive better than other albino animals because
   a. they can eat without seeing.
   b. the sun does not reach them.
   c. their enemies cannot see them.

5. A gray kitten with pink eyes and ears has
   a. a normal amount of melanin.
   b. less than a normal amount of melanin.
   c. no melanin at all.

6. When hunted by its enemies, a wild albino animal is more likely to be caught than a regular-colored animal because
   a. it is hard for a wild albino animal to hide.
   b. it is not easy for a wild albino animal to find food.
   c. a wild albino animal moves slowly.

The Spider—A Misunderstood Animal

How much do you really know about spiders?

Spiders are not insects. Insects have six legs and three body parts. Spiders have eight legs and two body parts. Of the 30,000 different kinds, or *species* (spē' shēz'), of spiders, only some spin webs.

All spiders produce "silk," but each species has its own way of using the silk. Spiders of one species, the web spinners, weave silky webs to catch their food, or *prey* (prā). The best-known web is the round web spun by the garden spider. Another species makes nets to drop over its victims. Another sends out a single sticky strand of silk like a fishing line to catch its food. When a fly gets stuck to the end of the line, the spider hauls in its "fish."

Web spinners seem to have three different life-styles. Some live by themselves in their webs. Others live in groups but have webs of their own for catching food. And still others live, hunt, and feed together off the same

web. Spiders that do not spin webs may hunt their prey or wait for their prey to come to them. Crab spiders, for example, will hide in flowers and wait for visiting insects.

Since they feed on insects, some spiders are considered "helpful." But spiders have no way of knowing whether or not an insect is a pest. In fact, when it comes to food, spiders are not choosy. They will eat anything that comes their way!

1. The word in the story that means "kinds" is _____.

2. To catch its prey, the "fishing" spider uses a
   a. round silk web.
   b. fishing line.
   c. single silk thread.

3. According to the story, all spiders
   a. are insects.
   b. spin webs.
   c. make silk.

4. Another title for this story might be
   a. Choosy Eaters.
   b. Interesting Insect-Eaters.
   c. Lonely Web Spinners.

5. What would a crab spider most likely be doing in among the petals of a flower?
   a. getting its rest
   b. waiting for its prey
   c. hiding from its enemies

6. Under which heading would you put garden spiders?
   a. Web Spinners
   b. Hunting Spiders
   c. Fishing Spiders

Listen to the Peepers

You need sharp eyes to spot these tiny night singers.

A spring peeper is a tiny tree frog. A frog is an *amphibian* (ăm fĭb'ē ən), an animal that usually spends part of its life in water and the rest on land. Frogs make their homes just about anywhere there is fresh water. Like most amphibians, frogs are very active at night, when the humidity is high and their skins are not in danger of drying out.

On spring nights, male peepers gather near ponds and other wet places. The bubble, or air sac, under each frog's throat swells and deflates like a tiny balloon. When this happens, a noise is produced. The males use this noise to call the female frogs. The calls are a series of whistles about a second apart and can be heard more than a kilometer away!

The female tree frog lays jelly-covered eggs and attaches them to a plant on the edge of the pond. There may be as many as 2,000 to 8,000 eggs. About nine days later, many of these eggs hatch and become tadpoles. Then, eight to ten weeks later, the surviving tadpoles develop into frogs.

The mature tree frog has suckers on the ends of its toes so it can hold onto branches and smooth surfaces. It also changes colors to imitate its surroundings. These remarkable little creatures are truly something to see and hear.

1. Animals that usually spend part of their lives in water and the rest on land are called _____.

2. The calls that a male tree frog uses to attract a female are a series of _____.

3. Why is it safer for frogs to go on land at night instead of during the day?
    a. They can hide in the dark.
    b. The humidity is higher.
    c. They are more active then.

4. What fills the balloon under the male frog's throat as he calls?
    a. air
    b. water
    c. eggs

5. Before an egg becomes a frog, it becomes a
    a. tiny balloon.
    b. peeper.
    c. tadpole.

6. When on land, the tree frog hides by
    a. becoming a tadpole.
    b. changing its color.
    c. inflating its sac.

More and More Plants

Have you ever wondered how plants produce other plants?

Pollen (pŏl'ən) is a yellow powder that contains the male cells of plants. It is found on stalk-like parts of the plant called *stamens* (stā'mənz). Then, when pollen is carried to the *pistils* (pĭs'təlz), or female parts, of the plant, *pollination* (pŏl'ə nā'shən) takes place. Pollination is the way in which plants are fertilized. In order for most plants to reproduce or make new plants, pollination is necessary.

Pollination can take place in many ways. The wind helps pollinate corn. The stamens of the corn plant grow above the leaves, and the wind blows the pollen from the stamens onto the pistils.

Sometimes the stamens grow inside the flowers of a plant. Insects help to pollinate these plants. The monarch butterfly, for example, feeds on milkweed nectar. While the butterfly is feeding, its legs get covered with pollen. When the butterfly moves to other milkweed plants, some of the pollen comes off its feet. The pollen lands on the plants' pistils and fertilizes them.

People who have orchards often use hand-pollination. They do this only with healthy trees. The pollen from these trees is collected and placed, by hand, on the pistils of other healthy trees. Hand-pollination usually results in larger and better-tasting fruit. With this method, the pollination is not simply left to chance.

1. In order for most plants to reproduce, or make new plants,
    _____ must take place.

2. The female part of a plant is called the
    a. stamen.
    b. pollen.
    c. pistil.

3. The pollination of corn is sometimes carried out by the
    _____.

4. Compared to hand-pollination, the pollination of milkweed is
    a. left to chance.
    b. carefully controlled.
    c. done by the wind.

5. Why does hand-pollination result in bigger and better crops?
    a. It is faster than waiting for the wind to do it.
    b. The pollen ripens faster.
    c. Only healthy trees are selected as parents.

6. Under which heading might you classify a plant that is
    pollinated by bees?
    a. Wind-Pollination
    b. Insect-Pollination
    c. Hand-Pollination

The Kudzu Vine

This plant is a real creeper.

In 1876, an interesting plant was brought over from Japan to the World's Fair in Philadelphia. It was the kudzu vine. Vines are plants with very long, rope-like stems. Vines usually grow along the ground, or climb a wall or some other support, by means of their *tendrils* (tĕn'drəlz). Tendrils are the thread-like parts of vines. The tendrils wrap around objects to hold up the vine's long stems.

Kudzu vines have long been a part of the scenery in southern parts of the United States. The vines grow well there thanks to the heat and humidity during the summer. People in the South began to put the kudzu to good use. They planted it on hillsides to keep the soil from washing away. And they planted it around houses to cover them and keep them cooler in the summer months. Before long, the kudzu had spread across the South. And people soon discovered that in places where the kudzu vine grew, other plants often could not grow. These vines grow quickly and deeply. They cover ground plants, bushes, and trees. If covered plants do not get sunshine for a long time, they will die. Farmers have tried to kill the kudzu with chemicals, but the treatment takes time and must be repeated.

Kudzu is used frequently in Oriental cooking, and it is considered healthful. Perhaps scientists will find other good uses for the kudzu in the future. If so, kudzu may become known as a helpful plant instead of a pest.

1. The thread-like parts of a vine that wrap around objects are called _____ .

2. People in the United States first saw the kudzu
   a. at the 1876 World's Fair.
   b. covering their hillsides.
   c. growing on houses.

3. In Japan, the kudzu is used
   a. to kill other plants.
   b. in cooking.
   c. to make silk.

4. What about the kudzu made it popular at first but eventually a problem?
   a. its long stems
   b. its fast growth
   c. the chemicals in it

5. Why do you think farmers wanted to kill the kudzu?
   a. Other crops cannot grow where the kudzu grows.
   b. Farm animals die if they eat it.
   c. It is expensive to grow and treat.

6. If the kudzu were planted in a cool, dry climate, it would probably
   a. kill the other plants.
   b. spread quickly.
   c. die out.

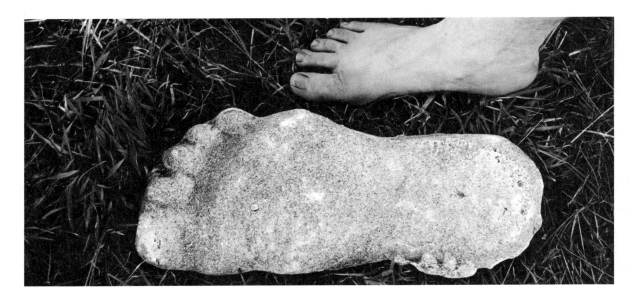

The Bigfoot Story

Have you seen a monster around lately?

Most of us have heard about Dr. Frankenstein's frightening *monster* (mŏn'stər). A monster can be imaginary, that is, not real. But it can also be a very large, or sometimes vicious, creature. Mary Shelley wrote the book in which Dr. Frankenstein created his monster. But that monster was not real. It was only something you read about in a book.

But what about a monster that goes by the name of Sasquatch, or Bigfoot? Over the years, many people claim to have seen it. Legends about the monster have been handed down from one generation to the next.

In 1958, some large, human-like footprints were found in northern California. Then, in 1967, a film was made. It showed what some people believed was the "Bigfoot" monster. In the film, a gorilla-like creature could be seen in the distance. Yet this large being was not shown up close.

In 1977, Bigfoot turned up in South Dakota. People claimed it was two or three meters tall. Its weight was described between 180 and 270 kilograms! In 1982, a forest ranger found footprints in Washington state that caused wider interest. The prints were over .5 meters long. They showed ridges just like those found on the soles of human feet.

Scientists say there really is no proof that such a monster exists. This is because, so far, Bigfoot has never been found. But the search for Bigfoot is still going on. And to those who claim to have seen it, Bigfoot is real.

1. In the story, the word that describes a very large, frightening creature is _____ .

2. Another name for Bigfoot is _____ .

3. The film showed very clearly how Bigfoot looked.
    a. True
    b. False
    c. The story does not say.

4. The film made in 1967 could not be considered proof of Bigfoot's existence because
    a. the creature in the film was only two meters tall.
    b. there were no clear close-ups of the creature in the film.
    c. Bigfoot does not look like the gorilla in the film.

5. Most scientists believe that Bigfoot
    a. must be real.
    b. probably does not exist.
    c. will never be found.

6. Which of the following would be the best proof to show whether or not Bigfoot exists?
    a. a photograph of the big creature
    b. a paw print of the big creature
    c. a drawing of the big creature

Elephants: A Struggle to Survive

Why are elephants struggling to survive in Africa?

Once, elephants were found all over Europe, Asia, and North America. Today, there are a few wild elephants in India, but only Africa has large herds of these six-ton animals. Yet, even in Africa, elephants are in danger.

For a long time, elephants have been hunted for their ivory tusks. The "white gold," another name for ivory, is used to make jewelry and carvings. In 1977, the government of Kenya passed a law banning elephant hunting. Half of the country's elephants had been killed off in five years. But the ban did not keep *poachers* (pō′chərz) from breaking the law. Some poachers kill the animals to get elephant tails for bracelets. Others only want heads to put on a wall.

But there is another, greater problem facing the African elephant. Every year there are more and more people in need of land to farm. An elephant eats about 135 kilograms of plants each day, and a herd may include as many as 100 elephants. There is just not enough land for both farmers *and* elephants to use. So African elephants must run from poachers and look for land on which to live.

All these elephants may be gone by the year 2000 if people continue to kill them for profit. A worldwide group is trying to stop this. Members of the group cannot protect all the elephants. So they chose several herds, about 250,000 elephants. Land is being provided for them. Poachers are being kept from the herds. If the elephants can grow old and die on the land, there will be enough ivory for all who want it. The herds will grow and future African elephants will be safe.

1. A person who hunts and kills animals that are protected by law is called a _____.

2. Large herds of wild elephants can still be found in _____.

3. An elephant can eat about six tons of plants each day.
   - a. True
   - b. False
   - c. The story does not say.

4. According to the story, the *main* reason elephants are hunted is that
   - a. their meat sells for a high price.
   - b. they are animals that cannot be tamed.
   - c. their ivory tusks are very valuable.

5. Why is there a problem between farmers and elephants?
   - a. Elephants are killing off some farm animals and driving cattle away.
   - b. Because of a shortage of grazing land, elephants are eating farmers' crops.
   - c. Farmers are paying hunters for bringing in elephant heads.

6. If you had to choose a newspaper headline to fit this story, which of the following would you choose?
   - a. Animal Herds without a Home
   - b. Poachers on the Run
   - c. Farmers Break the Law

A New Way to Use Old Tires

What can you do with worn-out automobile tires?

It is spring cleanup week in a small New England town. During this week, people set out their extra trash and old junk to be picked up by the trash collector. The townspeople were asked to separate out those pieces of trash that could be *recycled* (rē sī′kəld), or used over again. Recycling materials is a way of saving our resources from being all used up. Things such as old newspapers, glass bottles, and aluminum cans are brought to the town's recycling center. Trash that cannot be recycled goes to the town's trash center. But the townspeople discovered that there was one item which neither the trash center nor the recycling center would accept. Old automobile tires would not be picked up.

What, then, were people to do with their old tires? Some people in this small town really cared about bettering their environment. So they came up with another idea. Many of these *ecology* (ĭ kŏl′ə jē)-minded people were gardeners who did not like to waste things. So they found a way to use the automobile tires in the garden. First, they stacked two old tires together. Then, they filled the centers of each with garden soil and planted seeds in the soil. Soon, vegetables and flowers were sprouting from within these old tires. The townspeople had found a good way to reuse their old tires.

1. The process of using something over and over again is called
   _____ .

2. The people in this story who cared about improving their
   environment were _____-minded.

3. The small town asked its citizens to take their trash to the
   trash center.
   - a. True
   - b. False
   - c. The story does not say.

4. Before filling the used tires with soil, the gardeners had to
   - a. cut them up.
   - b. fill them with seeds.
   - c. stack them.

5. One reason that the town *probably* held spring cleanup week
   was to encourage people to
   - a. reuse everyday materials.
   - b. grow their own food.
   - c. throw out old junk.

6. Which of the following is *not* an example of recycling?
   - a. grinding glass to make new bottles
   - b. melting down scrap metal
   - c. burning old newspapers

A Study of Snoring

Why do some people snore?

Z-Z-Z-Z-Z-Z! That's how snoring looks in the comic strips! But snoring really is not very funny. People sometimes snore so loudly that they keep others around them awake. So snorers have tried different things to keep themselves from snoring. They have tied bandages from their chins to the tops of their heads so their mouths would stay shut during sleep. Doctors have even removed the *uvula* (yoō'vyə lə), a tab of soft tissue that hangs down from the roof of the mouth. In England, doctors also tried dropping pieces of soap into snorers' mouths whenever they snored. Sometimes turning over on one's side helps. But no one has yet found a way to completely stop this annoying sound.

Almost everyone snores at some time. But for some reason, men snore more than women and children. Snoring happens when the sleeper breathes through the mouth. This breathing in is called *inhalation* (ĭn'hə lā'shən). During inhalation, the air coming in causes either the soft *palate* (păl'ĭt) or the vocal cords to vibrate, or move rapidly back and forth. This makes a rattling, broken sound. Other parts of the mouth may also vibrate. Inhalation may cause the lips, cheeks, and nostrils to get dry. Then the vibration becomes faster and the snoring gets louder.

If you do not snore at all, you are lucky. If you have never snored before and suddenly begin to snore a great deal, something may be wrong. Then you should go to a doctor and be examined.

1. Another word for "breathing in" is _____ .

2. According to the story, which of the following is true?
   - a. Women snore more than men.
   - b. Children snore more than adults.
   - c. Men snore more than children.

3. If you suddenly develop a bad snoring problem, it would be best to
   - a. soap your mouth.
   - b. tie your jaw shut.
   - c. see a doctor.

4. The actual sound produced during snoring is caused by
   - a. parts of the mouth vibrating.
   - b. the sleeper trying to talk.
   - c. the lips and cheeks getting dry.

5. A person who snores always sleeps with his or her mouth
   - a. tied shut.
   - b. open.
   - c. vibrating.

6. When people who snore wake up in the morning, they probably
   - a. have a cold.
   - b. are thirsty.
   - c. slept well.

A Fearsome Snake

How dangerous is a boa constrictor?

Except for the shark, no animal causes fear in the hearts of so many people as does the boa constrictor. Many stories tell of adventures with this snake or its larger relative, the anaconda. Some people fear the boa because they think it is poisonous. But it is not. The boa constrictor kills its prey, or victim, by wrapping itself around the body of the animal and squeezing, or *constricting* (kən strĭkt′ĭng), it. When the boa constricts, it gets smaller. By wrapping itself tightly around its prey, the boa prevents the animal from taking in any air. Then the animal dies.

The boa constrictor does not chase its prey. Usually, a boa simply lies and waits for a small animal, such as a lizard, bird, or mouse, to pass by. Boas do not eat very often. Some eat only once a month and can wait even longer if they have to.

The size of a boa often frightens people. It can reach a length of 5½ meters. However, there have been reports of anacondas as long as 15¼ meters! In most cases, boas will not attack people. This is because people are much too big for them to eat. If an attack occurs, usually the boa cannot constrict itself enough to seriously harm the person.

Boa constrictors are found only in warm countries, in places like South America and Mexico. Boas that live in the United States are usually found in pet shops or zoos.

1. The word in the story that means to squeeze and get smaller is
   _____ .

2. The larger relative of the boa constrictor is the _____ .

3. In order to catch its prey, the boa constrictor _____ the
   animal.
   > a. chases
   > b. waits for
   > c. sneaks up on

4. The boa constrictor probably got its name from
   > a. its great length.
   > b. the way it kills its prey.
   > c. its poisonous tail.

5. Which of the following statements is *not* true?
   > a. Boas prefer to live in warm climates.
   > b. Boas are a serious threat to humans.
   > c. Boas can go for long periods without eating.

6. If you saw a boa wrapped tightly around another animal, you
   would know the boa was
   > a. taking a rest.
   > b. going to eat soon.
   > c. poisoning the animal.

The Damselfly

This beautiful insect has bright, flashing wings.

The damselfly is an insect that is usually found near water. It may stray for a while but will return to its home waters to mate and lay its eggs. The *life cycle* (līf′ sī′kəl) of the damselfly has three stages: the egg, the nymph, and the winged-adult. This life cycle, or series of changes, is usually about one year long.

Damselflies mate while in flight over water. A few minutes later, the female drops her eggs into the water or inside the stems of water plants. The damselfly has enemies, such as birds and fishes and sometimes other insects and frogs. So, while the female may lay hundreds of eggs at one time, she never drops more than a dozen eggs in any one spot.

A young damselfly, or *nymph* (nĭmf), hatches from the egg in about one week. During this stage, it spends its life under water, where it eats water insects and sheds its skin as it grows. After several months, the nymph is ready to become a winged-adult. Crawling from the water, it sheds its last nymph skin. In one or two hours, its wings spread and harden, and it is ready to fly.

The body of the winged-adult is a shiny blue or green. The male's wings are brightly colored. The female's wings are usually clear but have brightly colored markings. Like the butterfly, the damselfly folds its wings over its back when it rests.

1. The damselfly is called a nymph in the _____ stage of its life cycle.
    a. first
    b. second
    c. third

2. Why does the damselfly return to its home waters?
    a. to shed its skin and die
    b. to mate and lay its eggs
    c. to hunt for food

3. The story compares the damselfly to the butterfly in terms of the
    a. bright color of their wings.
    b. way they fold their wings.
    c. way they lay their eggs.

4. How often does the damselfly shed its skin?
    a. never   b. only once   c. several times

5. After spending a couple of months in the water, the damselfly is ready to
    a. lay its eggs.
    b. hunt for insects.
    c. shed its nymph skin.

6. Why does the female damselfly drop no more than a dozen eggs in one spot?
    a. She never produces more than a dozen at one time.
    b. She wants to make sure that at least some will hatch.
    c. She flies too fast to drop them all in the same spot.

Save the Tigers

A gun sounds. A loud crash is heard. Then there is silence.

Chuchchi is a *tigress* (tī′grĭs), a female tiger. The tigress is not dead, only asleep. Chuchchi has been shot with a drug-bearing dart. The hunters are scientists who are part of a worldwide study to save *endangered* (ĕn dān′jərd) animals. Endangered animals are animals that are in danger of dying out. Scientists are trying to learn enough about the habits of these endangered animals to make sure that they have a future.

Quickly, the scientists set to work. A pillow is placed under Chuchchi's head. Her body is soaked with water to bring down her temperature, which may go up from the drug. Then, the number 115 is marked on her ear. The tiger, like all animals in this study, has been given a series number. Both male and female tigers are marked with a number from 101 to 199. Chuchchi is the 15th tiger to be marked. Next, a collar is placed around her neck. Each tiger collar sends out a radio signal. The scientists carry a radio receiver. Then, when they hear Chuchchi's signal, they will be able to identify and locate the tigress.

Pictures are taken of the stripes on Chuchchi's face and the tracks left by her paws. The paw prints and face stripes of each tiger are different from those of other tigers. So the pictures will help to identify Chuchchi.

1. A female tiger is called a _____.

2. An animal that is in danger of dying out is said to be _____.

3. What two characteristics of tigers are different for each tiger?
   _____

4. The number 115 shows that Chuchchi is
   - a. 115 years old.
   - b. The 5th tiger collared.
   - c. The 15th animal in the study.

5. Read the following sentences. Then number the sentences to show the order in which the scientists did their work.
   - ____ a. Chuchchi was shot with a drug-soaked dart.
   - ____ b. A radio collar was put around the tigress's neck.
   - ____ c. The tigress was soaked with water to lower her temperature.

6. Why do scientists want to be able to identify these animals?
   - a. So they can take pictures of them.
   - b. So they can study their habits.
   - c. So they can put them to sleep.

Does a Sea Animal Keep a Diary?

A sea animal called the nautilus has a beautiful swirled shell around its soft, worm-like body.

When the *nautilus* (nôt′l əs) dies, its shell is left behind. Sometimes this shell washes up on the seashore. If you find one and hold it up to your ear, you can hear the sound of the sea. One scientist believes that the nautilus's shell may be a measure of time. This means that as the animal built its shell, it left behind a kind of mark for each day that it lived.

The nautilus's shell is like a tube around its body. As the nautilus grows, the tube gets bigger, layer by layer, twisting around in a coil. Every so often, the nautilus walls off the old part of the shell and moves into the new part it has just made. The part that has been walled off is called a *chamber,* another word for a room. By studying many shells, the scientist has found that there are usually 30 layers of shell in each chamber. There is no proof yet, but the layers of shell may have been made one day at a time.

If this theory is true, then it would be possible to tell how long the nautilus lived simply by counting the layers in its shell. It could be that this famous sea animal's beautiful shell is a diary, after all. The shell may be a measure of time, and it may tell us a lot about the time during which the nautilus lived.

1. In the story, the name of the sea animal with a soft, worm-like body is the _____.

2. The part of the sea animal's shell that has been walled off is called a _____, or room.

3. As the sea animal gets bigger, its shell
    a. cracks.
    b. grows.
    c. falls off.

4. If the scientist can prove that the animal added a layer to its shell each day, that means that
    a. the shell can be used as a measure of time.
    b. the animal grows the same amount each day.
    c. the animal has lived 365 days.

5. The nautilus lives in which part of its shell?
    a. in the part sealed off as a chamber
    b. in the new part made after a chamber is sealed off
    c. in the entire length of the shell

6. Suppose you found a nautilus's shell on the beach and you counted the layers in the shell's chambers. You would most probably find that each chamber was equal to one _____ time.
    a. day's
    b. month's
    c. year's

Fish That Will Not Freeze

A South Pole fish gets a blood test.

In the freezing sea near Antarctica, the water is so cold that it is often filled with tiny crystals of ice. Yet the fish that live in this water do not freeze. Why?

To find the answer, one scientist made three basic tests on the fish's blood. First, he looked through a microscope at the blood sample. He was surprised to find that, unlike other fish, these fish had no red blood cells! Red blood cells carry oxygen to other body cells. Yet enough oxygen circulates in the South Pole fish to keep them healthy. How is this possible? The answer could help doctors make sure that enough oxygen is circulating through a patient's bloodstream during surgery.

Next, the scientist wanted to find the freezing temperature of the fish's blood. He put a few drops of blood in a small test tube and put the tube in a special cooling pan. Then he measured the temperature at which the fish's blood froze and discovered that it froze at temperatures far below that of the water in which the fish lived!

Lastly, he did a chemical test on the fish's blood. The test showed that there was a chemical, like antifreeze, in the blood. Antifreeze is a mixture that lowers the freezing point, or temperature at which a liquid freezes. This keeps ice crystals from forming. It is not surprising, then, that this fish that will not freeze is called the ice fish.

1. A chemical mixture that prevents a liquid from freezing at certain temperatures is called _____.

2. The fish that will not freeze is called the _____.

3. The freezing point is best described as
    a. the temperature at which a liquid freezes.
    b. the temperature of antifreeze.
    c. the temperature of water and antifreeze mixed.

4. How would you compare the ice fish to other fish?
    a. Other fish have red blood cells.
    b. The blood of the South Pole fish contains no oxygen.
    c. The blood of other fish contains antifreeze.

5. Number the following actions in the order in which they occur in the story.
    ____ The blood sample was put in a cooling pan.
    ____ The temperature of the blood sample was measured.
    ____ The fish's blood was put in a test tube.

6. Pretend you are a doctor. You are about to perform an operation on a patient. Which of the following things should you watch out for during the operation?
    a. the number of blood cells in the patient's body
    b. the flow of oxygen through the patient's bloodstream
    c. the amount of antifreeze flowing through the patient's bloodstream

Aspirin

Cold Capsule

Cough Syrup

Willow Bark

Chamomile

Mint

Old Ways Can Work

Can plants be considered medicine?

Willow bark, witch hazel twigs, foxglove leaves, yam roots, and quinine were once used to cure sickness. But today's medicines are mostly *synthetic* (sĭn thĕt'ĭk). Synthetic medicines are medicines that are made from chemicals. Sometimes these medicines come in the form of pills, powders, or pleasant-tasting liquids. But old and new medicines are not as different as they may seem.

Studies have proved that in some ways folk medicines are similar to modern drugs. For example, to relieve fevers, colds, and stiff joints, Native Americans used willow-bark tea. Its chemical content is much like aspirin. The Incas of Peru had a remedy

for malaria (mə lâr'ē ə), a disease. They used cinchona bark, or quinine. Unlike today's synthetic quinine, cinchona bark was effective against all types of malaria.

A Mexican folk cure recommended yam-root tea for *arthritis* (är thrī'tĭs), a disease that affects the joints in the body. And today, one of the modern drugs used to treat arthritis contains a synthetic ingredient that can be traced back to yam roots.

Research into folk medicine continues. Doctors know that they cannot completely ignore folk medicines. But it is necessary to carefully separate the useful folk remedies from those that could be dangerous.

1. The word in the story that describes something made from chemicals is _____ .

2. Which of the following folk medicines is chemically similar to aspirin as we know it?
   a. foxglove leaves
   b. quinine
   c. willow-bark tea

3. The Incas used cinchona bark to help cure _____ .

4. According to the story, which of the following statements is true?
   a. Doctors now are using folk medicines to cure most illnesses.
   b. Folk medicines can be unsafe and must be used carefully.
   c. The folk medicines used long ago were never effective against disease.

5. The Mexicans must have known that yam roots
   a. could relieve pain in the joints.
   b. would someday be a modern drug.
   c. could be used against all types of malaria.

6. Under which heading would you list yam root, witch hazel twigs, and willow bark?
   a. Synthetic Drugs
   b. Nature's Medicines
   c. Cure-Alls

Song of the Sea

What weighs thousands of kilo-grams, does back flips, blows bubbles, and sings?

The humpback whale is a huge sea *mammal* (măm'əl). Mammals belong to the group of animals that have hair or fur on their bodies. The females of the group produce milk for their babies. The whale is an unusual mammal because most mammals live on land.

The humpback is just one species, or kind, of whale. It lives in cold ocean waters during the summer and warmer waters in the winter. Usually these mammals move slowly through the water, either alone or in herds. But they can move fast if they are in danger from hunters or killer whales.

The humpback whales seem to be the only whales that sing. They sing only in their *breeding grounds* (brē'dĭng groundz), those parts of the sea where they gather to mate and have babies. They sing for six months of the year, and each song may last from 10 to 30 minutes.

Katherine and Roger Payne of the New York Zoological Society have been studying the songs of the whales for 22 years. Their studies show that there is actually a pattern, or plan, to the songs and that the whales change their songs each year. Research also shows that humpback whales move from one place to another.

Identifying the whales by their songs will help scientists keep track of how many humpback whales there are and where and how they live.

1. What word describes the group of animals that have hair or fur on their bodies and whose female members produce milk for their babies? _____

2. In order to mate and have babies, whales go to _____.

3. Each year, the humpback whales change their songs.
   - a. True
   - b. False
   - c. The story does not say.

4. According to the story, one enemy of the humpback whales has been
   - a. humans.
   - b. disease.
   - c. sharks.

5. Which of the following statements is *true?*
   - a. The humpback is one species of whale that has no speed.
   - b. Most humpback whales live in cold waters year round.
   - c. The humpback whale is an unusual mammal because it lives in water.

6. The story suggests that the song of the humpback whale would *best* be classified as a
   - a. hunting song.
   - b. noisy song.
   - c. mating song.

Too Much Sugar in Your Diet?

Most of the useless calories we eat come from refined sugar.

A *calorie* (kăl′ə rē) is a unit of measure. Calories are used to measure heat or energy. Nutritionists, or food experts, use calories to measure the energy value of the foods we eat. They have discovered that almost 20 percent of the calories in foods eaten by young people in the United States are useless. These foods contain none of the vitamins, protein, or minerals we need to stay healthy. Most of these useless or empty calories come from refined sugar, or *sucrose* (sōō′krōs′).

When we think of sugar, we usually think of soda pop, candy, and rich desserts. But much of the sugar we eat is "hidden" in other kinds of foods.

Sucrose is often added to food products before they get to our tables. If you read the labels on the food packages in your kitchen, you will find that many foods contain this refined sugar. In fact, ketchup contains about 30 percent sugar. And some breakfast cereals contain more than 50 percent sugar.

Of course, we need sugar for energy. But we do not need such large amounts of sucrose. Fruits and vegetables contain a better, more natural sugar called *fructose* (frŭk′tōs′), or fruit sugar. Fructose is better for our teeth and supplies us with all the energy we need. So watch your intake of sugar. You may be eating much more than you need.

1. The unit used to measure the energy value of our food is called the _____.

2. We need some sugar in our diet because it supplies us with
   a. vitamins.
   b. protein.
   c. energy.

3. Food and diet experts are called _____.

4. The story leads you to believe that
   a. most packaged foods have no sugar added to them.
   b. most people have too much sugar in their diets.
   c. sucrose is needed for a well-balanced diet.

5. The story suggests that a good way to get the sugar we need is by eating foods that contain
   a. refined sugar.
   b. fructose.
   c. vitamins.

6. Read the following list of foods. Put an *F* on the line next to the foods that are high in fructose. Put an *S* next to those foods that are high in sucrose.
   a. ____ cola
   b. ____ peas
   c. ____ cake
   d. ____ apples
   e. ____ pizza

Scoliosis

A disease called scoliosis (sko'le o'sis) affects about 1 out of 25 teenagers.

Scoliosis is a side-to-side curve of the spine, or backbone. It can happen almost anywhere along the spine. Scoliosis may cause the spine to be shaped like a C (single scoliosis) or like an S (double scoliosis). The disease can start during childhood or in the teen years, and there are both mild and severe cases.

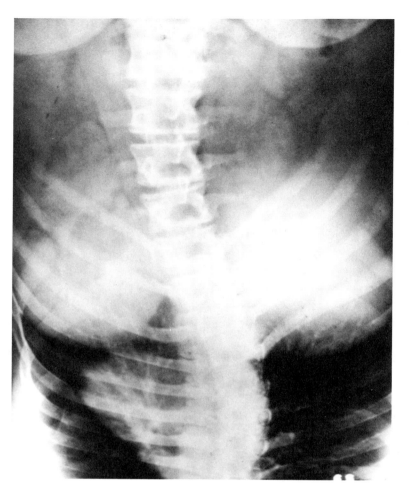

Mild cases of scoliosis are often caused by poor posture. These cases can be cured by exercise and correcting the way one walks and stands. More severe cases are often caused by an illness. In these more severe cases, braces can be used to correct the spine's curve. But sometimes an operation, or surgery, is required to correct the problem.

The side-to-side spine curving in scoliosis can create pressure on a person's ribs. This may cause the ribs to push against the heart and lungs. The effect can be very serious and result in illness and a shorter life. It is important, therefore, to begin treating the disease as early as possible.

With this in mind, the Scoliosis Research Society is encouraging a nationwide screening program to discover cases of scoliosis and other back problems. Trained persons will test 11- to 15-year-olds. They will be checking to see if shoulders are level, spines are straight, and hips are even, and to make sure that the entire back is in proper order.

1. Scoliosis is a disease that results in a _____ of the spine, or backbone.

2. A case of double scoliosis may make the spine look like the letter _____.

3. Some cases of scoliosis can be cured with the proper exercise.
   a. True
   b. False
   c. The story does not say.

4. According to the story, most cases of scoliosis can be cured
   a. quickly and easily.
   b. only in rare cases.
   c. when treatment starts early.

5. Pressure from the ribs can cause damage to the
   a. heart and lungs.
   b. shoulders and arms.

6. One way to avoid mild scoliosis is to
   a. wear braces.
   b. sit and stand up straight.
   c. have an operation.

Frank and John Craighead, Twin Brothers Who Study Wildlife

Drs. Frank and John Craighead are noted wildlife scientists. These twin brothers have studied, photographed, and recorded many of the sights and sounds of wildlife throughout North America. They spent several years studying grizzly bears in Yellowstone National Park in Wyoming.

Grizzly bears are meat-eating North American animals. They live in northern and western parts of the United States and Canada. Grizzlies are from 2 to 3 meters tall and weigh about 360 kilograms. For years, grizzlies were killed by hunters in many parts of North America and their number was greatly reduced. The Craigheads studied the grizzlies to find ways to help save the animals from extinction.

In Wyoming, the Craigheads captured grizzlies in special steel traps. After an animal was caught, it was given a drug to make it sleep. Then the scientists placed an ear tag on the bear for identification. The grizzly was weighed and measured, and special casts were made of the animal's teeth and paws. These casts showed the age of the bear. The picture above shows John Craighead taking prints of a grizzly's paw.

A special collar was attached to the bear. The collar had a radio transmitter that sent out signals which were picked up by scientists. So when the animal was released, the radio signals helped scientists keep track of the bear's whereabouts. From the Craighead study, much information has been learned about the habits of the grizzlies and why they should be protected.

Lake Erie Nature and Science Center

Explore a tide pool. Identify birds by their songs. Build a weather station. Touch a starfish. These are just a few of the things you can do at the Lake Erie Nature and Science Center in Cleveland, Ohio. The center is surrounded by woods, meadows, creeks, streams, and a lake.

The center was built in 1945 to help children and students gain more understanding of their environment. The center has many programs for students. One program deals with mammals that are found in Ohio. In class, children study the habits and characteristics of many different kinds of mammals.

Students can learn how to read simple and complex weather instruments. They learn to measure and record temperatures, humidity, and wind speed. They make weather forecasts and create a mini-tornado in the tornado machine. They can also build a weather station.

Students study about the oceans. They learn about different animals and plants that live in the sea. They

study saltwater food chains by observing live animals. Visitors can also see and pet animals in the outdoor animal yard.

Many students study the history of Lake Erie, which is nearby. They study about the plants and animals that live in and around the lake. They also study how pollution has affected the lake. Other programs deal with birds, trees, electricity, light, sound, and the human body.

Animals and Plants of the Ocean

Across

1. a soft-bodied animal having a fan-shaped shell
3. a large, air-breathing ocean mammal
5. a fish related to cod
7. an ocean mammal having a beak-like snout
8. an animal with eight arm-like tentacles
10. saltwater or freshwater mollusks
14. a simple water animal with a soft or bony skeleton
15. sea animals with tube-shaped bodies
17. any of the large brown seaweeds

Down

1. a green seaweed
2. an animal related to shrimp
4. a sea animal with paddle-like flippers
6. a sea animal with a star-shaped form
9. water animals that burrow into the soil
11. a large fish with sharp teeth
12. a large ocean fish caught for food
13. an ocean fish caught for food
16. a long, snake-like sea animal

Word List:

prawn, whale, scallop, kelp, eel, cod, starfish, sponge, hake, clams, tuna, octopus, dolphin, sea lettuce, seal, anemones, mussels, shark

The Human Body

See if you can find the names of 23 parts of the human body in the hidden puzzle game. The words go across, down, and diagonally. Use the word list if you need help.

```
S B L O O D S T L U N
K M U S C L E K L E E
L D N H A I R R U B G
I A G A R V E I N L A
G R A R T E R Y W A L
A M H H I R E A E D A
M B C E L S K I N D O
E W O T A N N O S E R
N I R N G R O N E R T
T I N V E R T E B R A
S K E L E T O N S E B
O C A P I L L A R Y A
```

Word List:

LEG, NOSE, HAIR, SKIN, EYE, LUNG, HEART, ARM, CORNEA, CAPILLARY, SKULL, CARTILAGE, BLOOD, SKELETON, BONE, BLADDER, AORTA, VERTEBRA, ARTERY, VEIN, LIVER, MUSCLE, LIGAMENTS

Investigating Extrasensory Perception

Imagine you are sitting in a math class. You just know the teacher is going to call on you. And sure enough, she does!

You get a feeling the phone is going to ring. And just then, it does!

You are at a friend's house watching TV. And all of a sudden you get a good feeling. Something wonderful has just happened. When you get home, you find out something wonderful. Your parents got you a new pet.

Your father calls you into the kitchen. Before he says a word, you know what he is going to say. And you are right!—"Please do the dishes tonight."

Coincidences? Well, maybe. In fact, probably. But then, maybe not. Maybe they are signs of ESP—extrasensory perception. ESP is the ability to know something without using your five senses.

In this set of science adventures, you will conduct some experiments. You are invited to determine your ESP abilities in three areas:

——— Clairvoyance
——— Telepathy
——— Precognition

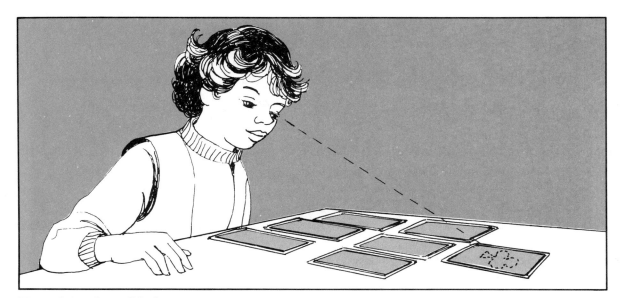

Testing for Clairvoyance

Clairvoyance is the ability to "see" something without using your eyes. In fact, you must not use any "normal" sense organ. Clairvoyance is being able to tell what is in a sealed envelope or box.

To do this experiment, you will need a deck of cards. Select 20 cards, other than aces. They will make up your ESP deck. Your deck should include five hearts, five clubs, five diamonds, and five spades.

Shuffle your ESP deck. Then place it face down on the table.

Take the four aces from the original deck. Place them in a face-up row in front of you.

Now you are ready to try the experiment. Try to guess the suit of each card in the ESP deck. Do not look at them. Take the top card in the deck.

Put it on the ace that you "see" is the same suit. Do the same for the remaining 19 cards.

After you are finished, turn over the four piles. Then tally your score. Give yourself one point for each correct placement.

Shuffle the deck and repeat the process four more times. That will make a total of 100 possible match-ups. Just by chance, you should be able to score 25 match-ups.

This experiment has been done with large numbers of persons. Here are the results. Only one person in 100 averages 36 correct match-ups. Only one in 1,000 gets 40 correct match-ups.

If you are that one person in 1,000, you are very unusual.

Testing for Telepathy

Telepathy is the ability to know what another person is thinking. It is the ability to "read" another person's mind.

To test for telepathic skills, you will need your ESP deck. You will also need a partner, a pencil, and paper.

Sit back to back with your partner. Have your partner look at the ESP deck. It should be looked at one card at a time. Your partner should concentrate on each card. The partner should try to send you a mental message: "This card is a club. This one is a heart."

You should try to "read" your partner's mind. Write down the suit you think each card is. Use C, D, H, and S for the suits. Your partner should also record what each card was. Each time you are ready, signal your partner: "Next card, please."

Shuffle the deck and repeat the process four more times. That will make a total of 100 possible correct guesses. Tally your score after each run through the ESP deck. The table below gives a rough estimate of your telepathic skills.

# CORRECT/100	TELEPATHIC SKILL
less than 25	You simply don't have it.
25	A "just-by-chance" score.
26-34	Maybe, just maybe, you've got some telepathic skills.
35 and above	Wow! You've got something!

Testing for Precognition

Precognition is the ability to sense or know something before it happens.

To check your precognition skills, you will need a partner. You will also need an ESP deck, paper, and a pencil.

Have your partner place the deck on the table. You try to guess the top card's suit. After each guess, your partner looks to check whether you are right or wrong. Repeat this process four more times. There will be a total of 100 possible correct predictions. Shuffle the deck after each run.

Evaluate your precognition skills with this table. (It is just like the telepathy table.)

# CORRECT/100	PRECOGNITION SKILL
less than 25	Your talents lie elsewhere.
25	A "just-by-chance" score.
26-34	It could be you have some precognition skills.
35 and above	Wow! Maybe you should be a fortune teller.

58

EARTH-SPACE SCIENCE

Weather balloons carry scientific instruments high into the air. The instruments measure the air's temperature, humidity, and pressure. The balloon also carries a radio that transmits the soundings, *or measurements, to ground stations. Scientists use the information to forecast the weather. The balloon in this picture has a special purpose. It is being used by environmental scientists to study the movement of pollution through the atmosphere.*

Weather Satellites

Satellites provide early warnings of dangerous weather conditions.

There are four weather satellites that *monitor* (mŏn′ĭ tər), or watch, changes in the earth's atmosphere. These include two polar-orbiting satellites and two stationary ones. The satellites carry instruments that "sense" energy from Earth and signal, or send, it back to weather stations. There the signals are turned into photos. The photos show a part of the earth, for example, North America. The white, cloudy areas in the photos show those places where the weather is overcast, or where rain may fall. The swirly, white areas show where storms, such as hurricanes, are and in what direction they are headed.

Weather forecasters, environmental scientists, and others depend on *data* (dā′tə), or information, gathered about weather conditions. A hurricane in the Atlantic, thunderstorms in Kansas, or a blizzard in Montana is carefully monitored. Over Florida, for example, satellites send back information on temperature every half hour. With early warnings, citrus growers and farmers can protect their crops from frost.

Sometimes the satellites detect trouble caused by human error. In 1979, shrimp-boat captains and wildlife specialists received information on giant oil slicks that threatened the Texas coastline. The rescue of wildlife and the protection of shrimp beds and tidal marshes depended on early warning. Luckily, it came in time.

QUESTIONS

1. The word in this article that means "to watch carefully" is _____ .

2. The information the satellites gather is called _____ .

3. Two types of satellites mentioned in the article are _____ and _____ .

4. In this passage, the *main purpose* of the satellites is to
   a. give early warnings of dangerous weather conditions.
   b. prevent frosts in farm areas.
   c. watch for shrimp boats.

5. It is important for wildlife specialists to be informed about oil slicks so they can
   a. take photos of the animals in the wildlife area.
   b. write an official report on wildlife damage.
   c. try to save the wildlife from total disaster.

Look at the weather satellite photo below. Then answer question 6.

6. Which number on the map shows the part of the United States that was in the most danger from Hurricane Anita on August 31, 1977?
   a. 1　　　　　b. 2　　　　　c. 3

The Greatest Show on Earth

It was daytime, yet total darkness had fallen over part of the earth.

Late in February 1979, the moon gave its last show of the century over parts of the United States and Canada. The moon moved directly between the earth and the sun, causing a total *solar eclipse* (sō′lər ĭ klĭps′). To eclipse is to block out or cover. During a total solar eclipse, the sun is blocked out by the moon and cannot be seen from certain parts of the earth.

People traveled great distances to see this event. Those who wanted to look at the sun used special glasses with very strong filters to protect their eyes. Slowly the moon passed directly between the sun and Earth. Then, the sun was blocked from view and the sky darkened, making it seem like nighttime. The shining ring of the sun's pinkish white *corona* (kə rō′nə) could be seen streaming out around the moon's edges. The corona is energy in the form of gases blasting out from the sun into space. Now only the corona was visible.

Animals must have noticed the eclipse, too. Cows, thinking it was night, headed for the barn. Dogs whimpered and birds went to sleep. After more than two minutes, the eclipse was over and it was daytime once again. A total solar eclipse is a rare sight, indeed. Not until the year 2017 will such a sight be seen again from the United States.

1. The shining ring of light streaming out from the sun is called its _____ .

2. When will the next solar eclipse be visible from the United States?

3. Where is the moon during a total solar eclipse?

4. The cows probably headed for the barn during the eclipse because they
   a. were afraid.
   b. wanted to be milked.
   c. thought it was nighttime.

5. Why were special glasses worn by some people?
   a. to block out the sun's burning rays
   b. because they couldn't see in the dark
   c. to protect themselves from the moon's glare

6. A word meaning "of the moon" is *lunar* (lōō′nər). Based on what you have learned in the story, what is meant by a *lunar eclipse*?
   a. The sun is blocked out by the moon.
   b. The moon is blocked out by the earth.
   c. The earth is blocked out by the moon.

Lightning—A Bolt from the Sky!

Scientists are learning more about the bolts from the sky.

"It wasn't raining, just kind of dark and cloudy," the boy remembered. "I was playing third base and the batter had just struck out. Next thing I remember is waking up in the hospital."

The boy had been hit by *lightning* (līt'nĭng), a discharge, or release, of electrical energy from a cloud. The lightning had melted a chain around his neck, torn his cap, and heated up his belt buckle. Luckily, the boy escaped with only a few slight burns. But each year about 600 people are killed by lightning.

Lightning begins in thick, high storm clouds. A charge of electricity builds up within these clouds. The charged clouds may be attracted to an opposite charge. When the opposite charge is in the ground below, a bolt of electrical current may flash from the clouds to the ground. Usually the lightning will strike the highest object

that will conduct, or pass, its electrical charge through the ground. Such an object might be a tree or might be a person standing in an open field.

Meteorologists are studying information gathered by weather satellites about lightning. They know that lightning occurs mostly over land and usually in the early evening. They hope to learn exactly what kinds of clouds make lightning. Then, when such clouds are seen, people can be warned ahead of time—*before* the lightning strikes.

1. Lightning is a discharge, or _____, of electrical energy from a cloud.

2. Why wasn't the boy killed by the lightning?
   - a. He was wearing a chain.
   - b. It was early evening.
   - c. The story doesn't say.

3. Where does lightning begin?

4. Which of the following statements best expresses the *main idea* of the story?
   - a. Warning people about lightning is a useless effort.
   - b. Lightning is a very real danger.
   - c. Scientists are trying to stop lightning from occurring.

5. Sometimes lightning passes from one cloud to another. In order for this to happen,
   - a. the clouds must hold opposite electrical charges.
   - b. one cloud must be close to land and the other over water.
   - c. the clouds must be over an open field.

6. Which of the following would be the *most* dangerous place to be when lightning strikes?
   - a. under a tall tree
   - b. in a ditch
   - c. down in a basement

Friends and Partners

Dogs and humans have been friends and partners for thousands of years.

Paleontologists (pā'lē ən tŏl'ə jĭsts) are scientists who study the remains of plants and animals that lived long ago. These remains, called fossils, often are found preserved in earth, rock, or clay. The oldest fossils of a dog found so far have been dated at about 14,000 years. Only the jaw and the teeth of this dog have been found. But paleontologists believe that they are the remains of a dog that lived during the Stone Age.

The Stone Age is the name used to describe the earliest known time in human history. The friendship between dogs and humans may have started back in the Stone Age, at least 15,000 years ago. The dog was probably very helpful to the Stone Age people. It may have helped them to become known as great hunters. Stone weapons and tools have been found that were made and used by the Stone Age people. Paleontologists know, therefore, that these early humans could think.

Paleontologists also know that, like us, Stone Age people could not pick up the scent of animals. The dog's ability to scent other animals made it useful to humans. Stone Age people used the dog to help them hunt for food. The dog also protected them and their families. In return, these early humans offered the dog food and shelter. And so, dog and human became friends and partners.

1. Scientists who study the remains of plants and animals that lived long ago are called _____.

2. The oldest dog fossils found so far have been dated at _____.

3. The Stone Age people became known as great _____.

4. According to the story, scientists know that Stone Age people were able to think because
   a. they have found stone weapons and tools made by these people.
   b. these early humans made friends with the dog.
   c. fossils of people from the Stone Age have been found.

5. What special ability do dogs have that humans do not have?
   a. Dogs have the ability to find other animals by following their tracks.
   b. Dogs have the ability to pick up the scent of other animals.
   c. Dogs are able to live without food for a long time.

6. The story tells something about the Stone Age and the people who lived at that time. After the Stone Age came the Bronze Age. Why do you think this age in time is called Bronze?

Underwater Archaeology—A New Science Is Born

One hundred feet below them was an ancient wreck.

The year was 1960. The eight team members were divers and scientists. The ancient wreck was buried in the sands below the warm coastal waters off Turkey. Underwater *archaeology* (är′kē ŏl′ ə jē) was about to be born.

Archaeology is the study of ancient life, or how people lived thousands of years ago. The work of the archaeologist is to find and recover objects made by these ancient people and figure out how the objects were used.

The archaeologists on the team that found the ancient wreck usually worked on dry land. They knew the scientific methods used in dry-land archaeology. By adapting, or changing, these methods, the archaeologists could use them under water. After diving into the sea, the group used underwater cameras to take pictures of the wreck and its treasures. Next, they drew maps on plastic tablets to show where each object was located. Then, they used a tool that gently sucked the sand away from the treasures. Large objects were placed in baskets, which were brought up to the surface. Very heavy objects were pulled up with the aid of a balloon.

The recovered objects were put in a museum in Turkey. Archaeologists then brought the photos, drawings, and maps to the United States for further research. After seven years of study, the scientists learned that the wreck was 3,200 years old.

1. The study of how people lived thousands of years ago is called
   _____ .

2. The underwater methods used were _____ those of dry-
   land archaeology.
         a. adapted from
         b. totally different from
         c. exactly like

3. In order to pull heavy objects to the surface, the team used a
         a. boat.
         b. basket.
         c. balloon.

4. What did the scientists make first but use last?
         a. a machine to suck away sand
         b. photos and drawings
         c. balloons to lift the treasures

5. According to the story, underwater archaeology began
         a. 3,200 years ago.
         b. in 1960.
         c. almost seven years ago.

6. Under which heading would you look to find more information
   on objects like those found in this story?
         a. Methods Used in Dry-Land Archaeology
         b. Ancient Shipwrecks and Archaeology
         c. The Science of Archaeology

The Quicksand Story

How can you get out of quicksand?

Quicksand is a bed of loose, deep, fine soil mixed with water. It usually forms on the bottom of certain streams or riverbeds and along the shore. When it is dry, quicksand may look like powder, because its grains are round instead of jagged like the grains of regular sand. When wet, quicksand cannot support heavy weight, because it is loose and gives in easily to pressure.

Quicksand isn't only sand. It can be any kind of fine, loose soil, like mud or pebbles. When water flows through quicksand, the water pushes upward and causes the soil to push apart and swell. Each grain of soil then floats on a cushion of water. A person can sink very quickly in this shifting mass of loose soil.

Quicksand can be difficult to see. It may be covered with water, leaves, or grass. But being caught in quicksand is not hopeless. Quicksand will *not* suck a person down completely. In fact, it is possible to float on quicksand just as on water.

Some basic rules to remember if you step into quicksand are: remain calm; drop anything you are carrying to make your body lighter; stretch out your arms and lie flat on your back so that your body can float; very slowly begin to roll off the sand to firm ground. Give the quicksand time to flow around you. It may take hours to roll out. Just remember that the quicksand will act like water if you give it time.

1. Quicksand can be any kind of loose, deep, fine _____ mixed with water.

2. Regular sand grains are _____, while quicksand grains are _____.
   a. jagged, round
   b. square, round
   c. smooth, rough

3. When water mixes with quicksand, it causes the soil to
   a. sink.
   b. swell.
   c. tighten up.

4. According to the story, what is the *first* thing you should do after stepping into quicksand?
   a. Try to get out immediately.
   b. Bring your arms in close to your body.
   c. Stay calm.

5. How would you compare quicksand with water?
   a. A person can float on both quicksand and water.
   b. Unlike water, quicksand does not move.
   c. Heavy objects can float on quicksand but not on water.

6. Under which of the following headings would you list quicksand?
   a. A Hopeless Trap
   b. Loose, Shifting Soil
   c. A Sparkling Powder

Dams

You may live in an area where people can swim, water ski, fish, or sail all because of a dam.

A *dam* is like a wall that is built across a waterway to control the flow of the water. For many years, dams were built only of earth and rocks. Today, many dams are built of concrete.

When a dam is built, water is trapped and held behind the dam. This water forms a lake. The lakes can be used for recreation or for irrigating, or watering, crops. The lakes also provide *potable* (pō′tə bəl) water, water that is safe for drinking. This potable water is piped from the lake into houses and other buildings. The lake water further serves as a home, or *habitat* (hăb′ĭ tăt′), for fish and waterfowl.

Dams are often built to provide flood control. Just before the rainy season, the water in the dam is allowed to flow out very slowly. This lowers the water level in the lake so that snowmelt and rainfall can be stored there each spring and used as needed during the rest of the year.

Some dams are built to use the power of falling water to make electricity. Such dams have powerhouses that contain machines—turbines and generators. Water falls from the lake to the river below the dam. As the water falls, it is sent through the powerhouse. There, the force of the water turns the turbines and generators and produces electrical power needed to light and heat buildings.

1. The word used to describe water that is safe for drinking is
    _____ .

2. The lakes formed by dams provide water for irrigation.
    a. True
    b. False
    c. The story does not say.

3. According to the story, dams are built for different reasons.
    But *all* dams
    a. control the flow of water.
    b. are built of earth and rocks.
    c. provide electrical power.

4. If the water level in the lake behind the dam is *not* lowered
    before the rainy season, then the
    a. water in the dam will flow out too slowly.
    b. snow-melt and rainfall might cause a flood.
    c. lake will probably dry up.

5. When dams are built to provide electricity, which of the
    following happens *first*?
    a. Water is sent through the powerhouse.
    b. Water pressure turns the turbines and generators.
    c. Water falls from the lake to the river below the dam.

6. Suppose you owned a farm in a place where there was not much
    rainfall. How might a dam be *most* helpful to you?

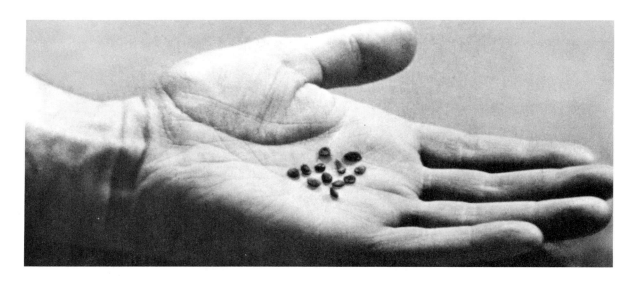

Tektites—From Earth or the Moon?

Where do tektites come from?

Large numbers of small, glass-like objects called *tektites* (těk'tītz') have been found in several parts of the world. They have been discovered both on land and under the waters of the oceans. Places in North America where tektites have been found are Georgia, Texas, and Martha's Vineyard in Massachusetts. Most tektites are round or tear-shaped and are dark brown or green in color. And they can be from 10 to 30 million years old.

Scientists aren't sure where tektites come from. But they have suggested four *theories* (thîr'ēz) about their origin, or beginnings. A theory is an idea scientists have that is based on some information, or evidence, that they have collected. Two theories suggest that tektites come from our moon. One moon theory is that, at some time in the past, a large meteorite struck the moon's surface and many of its glass-like pieces found their way to Earth.

The second moon theory is that, at some time in the past, a large volcano erupted on the moon. The explosion blew material from the moon out into space and onto the earth. In fact, the material in tektites is similar to certain volcanic material.

The last two theories suggest that tektites originated on Earth. One theory is that a meteorite hit Earth and produced tektites. Another says they formed from a volcanic eruption on Earth. Where do you think tektites come from?

1. An idea that is based on a collection of information or evidence is called a _____ .

2. So far, tektites have been found only on land.
   a. True   b. False   c. The story does not say.

3. If one of the moon theories were correct, then scientists would know that tektites were formed when a
   a. planet once hit our moon.
   b. meteorite once struck the earth's surface.
   c. volcano once erupted on our moon.

4. Which of the following might have happened first?
   a. Glass-like objects were found on Earth.
   b. A meteorite struck the moon.
   c. Bits of glass-like material flew out into space.

5. At the present time, tektites would be classified as being
   a. moon-made.
   b. Earth-made.
   c. of unknown origin.

6. Read the following list of words. Based on what you have read in the story, put an X in front of the word or words that would be used to describe tektites.
   _____ ancient
   _____ many-colored
   _____ glass-like bits
   _____ huge
   _____ volcanic-like material
   _____ few in number

The Mastodon Find

How do we know that relatives of today's elephants lived in North America thousands of years ago?

An exciting discovery was made in the state of Washington a few years ago. A pair of *tusks* were found in a peat bog. Tusks are long, pointed teeth that stick out of the mouths of certain animals, such as the elephant. These tusks, however, were unusually long. Scientists checked out the discovery and reported that the tusks were actually *fossils* (fŏs′əlz). Fossils are the remains of ancient plants and animals.

The scientists did some more digging and found many bones. The bones and the tusks were the remains of an ancient animal, the *mastodon* (măs′tə dŏn′). This relative of today's elephant was once common over much of North America about 11,000 to 14,000 years ago. Mastodons stood about 3 meters high and were covered with coarse, or rough, hair. They are *extinct* (ĭk stĭngkt′) now; that is, they no longer live on Earth.

Among the fossils found in Washington, scientists also discovered the sharp head of a spear. No one had ever before found a weapon buried with a mastodon. Now, scientists had evidence that mastodons may have been hunted by humans.

Mastodon fossils have been found in over 1,000 places, mostly wooded areas. Some scientists believe that mastodons were tree feeders, feeding on trees such as spruce, larch, and hemlock. Some mastodon fossils have even been dug up with hemlock twigs still sticking to their teeth!

1. Animals that no longer live on Earth are said to be _____.

2. Mastodons can still be found roaming parts of North America.
   a. True
   b. False
   c. The story does not say.

3. Why were scientists so interested in looking at the tusks found in Washington State?
   a. Mastodon tusks had never before been found.
   b. The tusks were unusually long.
   c. The tusks belonged to a modern-day elephant.

4. What did the discovery of a spearhead prove?
   a. Mastodon tusks were used as spearheads.
   b. Humans must have hunted mastodons.
   c. Mastodons lived off trees to survive.

5. Most ancient mastodons probably lived in
   a. deserts.
   b. water.
   c. forests.

6. Finding a fossil is like
   a. unlocking a door to the past.
   b. discovering a new form of life.
   c. living in the future.

Uranus, a Distant Planet

The third largest planet in our solar system was discovered by accident.

In 1781, William Herschel looked through his telescope and thought he saw a comet. Herschel was a famous British *astronomer* (ə strŏn'ə mər). An astronomer is a scientist who studies the planets and other things in space. After months of study, Herschel found that what he had discovered was a planet. It was the seventh planet from the sun.

It was not until March 10, 1977, that astronomers discovered something else about Uranus. There were five rings circling the planet. One month later, other astronomers proved that Uranus had four more rings, bringing the total number of known rings to nine!

The rings of Uranus are narrower and darker-looking than those of the planet Saturn. Uranus's five main rings, for example, are only 3 to 100 kilometers wide. Saturn's rings are about 50,000 kilometers wide.

It is believed that each ring of Uranus is made up of stone-like pieces of matter and that each ring may have been a moon of Uranus some time in the past. Scientists think that something, perhaps an explosion, caused the moons to break apart. Then, the pieces from each moon formed a ring around the planet. When Voyager 2 visited Uranus in January, 1986, ten new moons were discovered. We now have proof that the planet has a total of fifteen moons.

1. Scientists who study the planets and the universe are called
   _____.

2. Compared with the rings of Saturn, Uranus's rings are
   _____ and _____-looking.

3. The latest rings of Uranus were discovered in
   a. March 1977.   b. April 1977.   c. March 1986.

4. Which of the following most probably happened first?
   a. The rings of Uranus were formed.
   b. Moons began to revolve around Uranus.
   c. Explosions caused some of Uranus's moons to break apart.

Use the table below to answer questions 5 and 6.

THE RINGS OF URANUS	
Name of Ring	**Distance from Uranus**
Kappa	42,029 kilometers
Iota	42,394 kilometers
Theta	42,660 kilometers
Alpha	44,835 kilometers
Beta	45,788 kilometers
Eta	47,290 kilometers
Gamma	47,732 kilometers
Delta	48,408 kilometers
Epsilon	50,848 kilometers

5. Which two rings of Uranus are farthest apart?
   a. Theta and Alpha
   b. Beta and Eta
   c. Delta and Epsilon

6. How far is it from Gamma to Uranus? _____

Great Masses of Ice

These solid masses of ice are beautiful and dangerous.

A *glacier* (glā'shər) is a huge, slowly moving body, or mass, of ice. Some glaciers form in high mountain areas where snow is very deep and never melts. Others, called polar glaciers, form around the North and South Poles. The largest of these polar glaciers covers Antarctica, the South Pole. This glacier is one and a half times as large as the United States (not counting Hawaii and Alaska).

In the polar areas, the snow builds up, layer upon layer. The pressure from this great weight causes the bottom layers of snow to change to ice. Each year, more snow falls on top of the ice layers. Soon the weight is heavy enough to cause the mass of ice to move very slowly.

When glaciers reach bodies of water, huge chunks of glacial ice break off and float away as icebergs. An iceberg is especially dangerous since most of it is hidden under water. Perhaps you have heard about the *Titanic,* the huge ship that sank in 1912. The *Titanic* was on its first voyage when it crashed into an iceberg. Many of the 2,200 passengers drowned.

Today, scientists are keeping a close watch on glaciers. One glacier they monitor is the Columbia Glacier near Valdez, Alaska. Scientists think that a large number of icebergs may drop off this glacier in the coming years. Ocean-going ships traveling in the area will have to be on the alert. Then, if possible, they can go around the iceberg and avoid crashing into it.

1. A huge, slowly moving mass of ice is called a _____.

2. Besides forming at the earth's poles, glaciers can form _____.

3. What happens when glaciers reach bodies of water?
   a. Floods occur.
   b. Snow falls.
   c. Icebergs form.

4. An iceberg is _____ glacier.
   a. a kind of
   b. a small piece of a
   c. larger than a

5. Glaciers are formed when snow
   a. is pressed to ice under its own weight.
   b. falls, melts, and refreezes.
   c. is hidden under cold water.

6. The captain of a ship is told that an iceberg lies ahead. After looking at the iceberg, the captain decides that it does not look very large, and the ship continues on course. Was this decision correct?
   a. Yes. The captain could see that the iceberg was small enough for the ship to pass by.
   b. No. An iceberg's true size is not visible above water.
   c. No. It is not possible for ocean-going ships to go around icebergs.

Life Inside L5

Imagine modern pioneers living in a giant soup can!

Many years from now, a group of people may board a spacecraft. They will head into space to live together in a new place, or *colony,* (kŏl'ə nē). After a few days, they will arrive at their new home, a colony called L5. L5 is the scientific name for the colony's position in space in relation to Earth and the moon.

At the L5 location, the force of *gravity* (grăv'ĭ tē) of the moon exactly balances the force of gravity of Earth. This balance keeps the space colony in a *stable,* or steady, orbit.

The colonists on L5 would feel weightless, as if they were floating.

To solve this "floating people" problem, L5 spins in space. This spinning provides the colony with a force that *feels like* the pull of gravity. This force gives the colonists a feeling of having weight, just as gravity does on Earth.

Inside L5, colonists will see many of the sights they left behind on Earth. There is also much work to do. Some people will be busy providing everyday necessities for human life. Solar engineers will be building sun power stations. In these stations, the sun's energy will be collected, changed into another form of energy, and sent back to Earth. This source of energy could be one answer to Earth's future energy needs.

1. On Earth, the force that pulls us to the ground is called

   _____ .

2. L5 will spin slowly to provide
   - a. a kind of gravity for the colony.
   - b. another source of energy for the colony.
   - c. protection for its colony.

3. L5 is a point located
   - a. half the distance between Earth and the moon.
   - b. where the pull of the moon equals the pull of Earth.
   - c. halfway between the moon and the sun.

4. L5 will get its name from its
   - a. position in space.
   - b. unusual shape.
   - c. source of power.

5. What problem on Earth may be solved by building solar power stations in space?
   - a. the energy shortage
   - b. the need for more space
   - c. our need for gravity

6. Under which heading would you list the word *gravity*?
   - a. A Colony
   - b. A Force
   - c. A Location

Guion Buford, Astronaut

When the space shuttle Challenger blasted off in 1983, Guion Buford was on board. He was the first Black American to fly in space.

Guy Buford was born in Philadelphia in 1942. As a boy he loved stories about aviation. His best school subjects were science and math.

School was not easy for him but he studied hard. He became the first black to attend Penn State's school of engineering. He received his degree in Aerospace engineering at 22 and later earned an M.A. and a Ph.D. While in school he joined the Air Force ROTC and after graduating he served as a pilot in Vietnam. Buford flew 144 combat missions. He received 13 medals and his first outstanding unit award.

A group of 35 astronauts were chosen for the space shuttle program in 1978. After training for four years for their work in space, Dr. Buford was one of the two mission specialists chosen for the 1983 flight.

Part of the shuttle's mission was to launch a communications and weather satellite. The information gathered is sent back to Earth. It helps scientists predict floods and other weather conditions. It also helps them improve phone and TV systems all over the world. Buford and Dale Gardner also did tests on cells while in flight. These experiments, begun on previous flights, are designed to help in the development of drugs to cure various illnesses such as diabetes and heart disease.

A Visit to the Boston Children's Museum

One of the most popular museums in Massachusetts is the Children's Museum in Boston. About 500,000 people visit the museum each year. More than half of the visitors are children.

The Children's Museum is one of the oldest children's museums in the United States. It was started in 1913 by a group of science teachers. They wanted visitors to the museum to touch and do rather than simply see and hear.

Visitors can do many things in the Exhibit Center. One program helps children learn how a computer works and how to use it. They can use the computer to play all kinds of games, such as tick-tack-toe. Children can even use the computer to control the movements of a robot.

Another popular exhibit is called Small Science. Here, children can learn about ancient tools and tool-making. They can use tools made of common materials, such as coffee cans, string, rocks, and nails. One popular tool is the pump drill. It is made from a broomstick, a nail, a piece of wire,

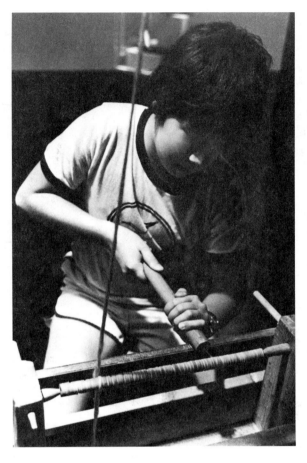

rocks, and some rope. Other tools include an ax and a wood grinder made of stone.

The Children's Museum has a large collection of rocks, fossils, shells, minerals, and reptiles. During the year, the museum has special activities, including making toys, flying kites, and learning about people from other countries.

Geology

Across

1. a land area with little rainfall
5. an icicle-shaped deposit hanging from the roof of a cave
6. a high, flat land area
8. molten rock beneath the surface of the earth
10. rocks formed by deposits of sediments
12. rock or snow that falls down a mountainside
15. an instrument that records earthquake waves
17. remains of animals and plants that lived long ago
18. the outer layer of the earth

Down

2. a giant ocean wave caused by an earthquake
3. a large, level surface of land
4. an island of coral
7. rocks and sand left by the melting ice of a glacier
9. rocks that have been changed by heat and pressure
11. rocks formed by hot, molten rock
13. a wearing away of the land
14. a flat top of land with steep cliffs
16. dark-colored material in the soil

Word List:

stalactite, erosion, humus, mesa, crust, sedimentary, avalanche, fossils, plain, tsunami, desert, seismograph, atoll, moraine, plateau, magma, metamorphic, igneous

Meteorology

Hidden in the puzzle below are 18 words that are related to weather or meteorology. The words go across, down, and diagonally. Use the words in the word list if you need help.

```
D W A T E R V A P O R
E F R O S T A T H B A
W I A R W E M H U L I
W I R N N I S U M I C
B S H A I L N N I Z L
R I M D I V O D D Z O
E N F O G N W E I A U
E I C E G F I R T R D
Z O S L E E T T Y D S
E B A R O M E T E R O
```

Word List:

CLOUDS, BREEZE, RAIN, SNOW, BLIZZARD, HAIL, SMOG, THUNDER, WATER VAPOR, DEW, BAROMETER, WIND, HUMIDITY, ICE, TORNADO, FOG, SLEET, FROST

Conserving Water

One of our most precious resources is fresh water. We need it for drinking, washing, and other activities. Like so many other resources, fresh-water supplies are limited. There is great need for water conservation.

In this science adventure, you learn to read your water meter. You will also keep a record of your family's water use. You should be encouraged to try to use less water.

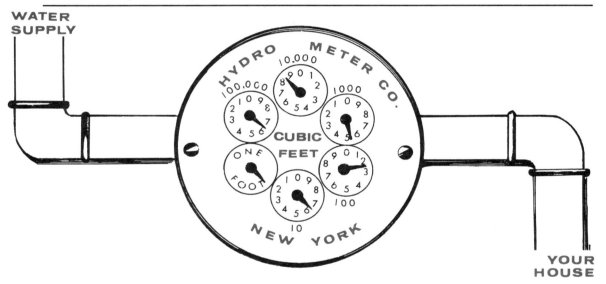

Reading a Water Meter The round meter shown here is the one most commonly used. It is not easy to read. The pointers on alternate dials move in opposite directions. Check the way the numbers are printed on each dial. That will help you to see which way the pointer moves.

To read the meter, begin with the "100,000" dial. Read each dial in order to the "10" dial. When the pointer is between numbers, always read the lower number. Do not read the "one foot" dial. It only shows if the meter is working. This meter shows readings of 6, 8, 5, 2, 6 (685,260 cubic feet).

Call your local water company. Ask them how much your family is charged for the water it uses.

Keep a record of your family's water use each day for a week. To find the water used each day, do the following: Subtract the reading of the day before from that day's reading. Day #1's reading minus the starting reading equals Day #1's water used. Day #2's reading minus Day #1's reading equals Day #2's water used. And so on.

	Starting Data	Day #1	Day #2	Day #3	Day #4	Day #5	Day #6	Day #7
Date								
Meter Reading								
Water Used Each Day								

CONSERVING WATER   Talk it over with your family. Try to get everyone to agree to conserve water for one week. Some things that can be done include:

- repairing leaky faucets
- adjusting leaky toilets
- taking shorter showers
- using less bath water
- shutting off water while brushing teeth and soaping up
- using a full load when you wash clothes or dishes
- using less water on lawns, gardens, and auto washing.

Keep a record of your family's water use during "conservation week."

	Starting Data	Day #1	Day #2	Day #3	Day #4	Day #5	Day #6	Day #7
Date								
Meter Reading								
Water Used Each Day								

By making some real efforts, how much water did your family save in a week? _____

How much money would your family save in a year if you conserved this much water every week? $_____

Investigating Water Evaporation

Evaporation is the process by which a liquid changes to a gas. Liquid water evaporates from the surface of the earth. It becomes an invisible gas, water vapor, in the atmosphere.

In this science adventure, you will investigate how four things affect evaporation.

• heat • surface area • wind • type of soil

For the first two activities, you will need four strips of blotter or filter paper (4 cm × 8 cm). You will also need thread, a fan, and water.

Hang each strip of paper from a piece of thread (about 20 cm long). Completely wet each piece of paper with water.

Heat

Place one piece of paper in the sunlight or in a warm place. Keep the other piece in a dark or cool place.

OBSERVATIONS: _____

_____

_____

Wind

Fan one piece of paper. You may use an electric fan. Or you may fan it with a rapidly moving piece of cardboard. Allow the other piece to hang undisturbed.

OBSERVATIONS: _____

_____

_____

Surface Area

Pour 100 ml of water into a large, flat container. A pie plate will do fine. Pour another 100 ml of water into a tall, narrow container. Try using an olive jar. Put the two containers in the same place in the room. That controls the effects of other variables, such as wind and temperature.

How much water is left in each container 4 hours later? 24 hours later?

OBSERVATIONS AND DISCUSSION: _____
_____
_____
_____
_____

Type of Soil

Get three large milk containers. They must all be the same size. Fill each with a different type of soil. Use sandy soil, clay, and rich, organic soil (loam). Pour one cup of water into each container. Weigh each container daily for a week.

OBSERVATIONS AND DISCUSSION: _____
_____
_____
_____

Weight of Soil

	DAY 1	DAY 2	DAY 3	DAY 4	DAY 5	DAY 6	DAY 7
SAND							
CLAY							
LOAM							

PHYSICAL SCIENCE

These four devices capture the natural energy of the sun and wind and turn it into power that people can use. The solar collector in the foreground tilts and rotates to follow the sun across the sky. The flat-plate solar collectors behind it do not move. They are spread out in a large, rectangular panel to catch the sun's rays. Behind the solar collectors stand two windmills. The modern turbine generator with three propellers converts wind power into electricity. The other windmill is the type once used to pump water on most farms in the United States. Today, as energy costs rise, many of these windmills are being used again.

Now We Have Cow Power

Even the barnyard can help produce energy.

These days, cattle are doing more than giving milk. They are also supplying energy. Energy made from cow waste, or *manure* (mə no͝or′), is being used to warm homes in at least one big city.

A company in Colorado makes a gas called *methane* (mĕth′ān′) out of cow manure. Methane will burn to make heat energy. Methane, like natural gas, is an important fuel. There are a lot of cows in Colorado. And so, there is a lot of cow manure. At present, the company buys the cow manure of over 100,000 cattle and hauls the manure back to its methane factory.

There, the solid part of the manure is removed. The liquid that is left is put into special tanks. There, *bacteria* (băk tîr′ē ə), or germs, feed on the liquid. As they feed, the bacteria turn the liquid into methane and other substances. The other substances are removed, and the methane is then sold to a gas company. The gas company sends the methane gas through a pipeline to homes and other buildings. The gas is used for heat and cooking.

But that is not all. The solid part of the manure is also used. It is treated and made into fertilizer and cattle feed. The feed is sold back to the cattle owners. Cows eat the food and make more manure. And the whole thing starts over again!

1. Methane is a kind of _____.

2. In this story, another word for cow waste is _____.

3. In what state is cow waste being used to make methane?
   _____

4. What must be present in order to turn liquid cow waste into methane?
   - a. natural gas
   - b. bacteria
   - c. fertilizer

5. What must be done *first* before methane can be made from cow waste?
   - a. Place the liquid part of the manure in a tank.
   - b. Treat the solid manure with other substances.
   - c. Separate the liquid part from the solid manure.

6. What is missing in the following chain of events?

| Solid manure is made into feed. | The feed is sold to cattle owners. | | Cows make more manure. |

The Light That Saves

A new energy-saving bulb lights the way.

Now that we must save energy, we need a new light bulb. You will know why if you have ever touched a light bulb that has been on for a while. The heat from the bulb is wasted energy.

The light bulb used in most homes is the *incandescent* (ĭn′kən dĕs′ənt) bulb. Incandescent means "glowing with heat." Inside the bulb is a thin wire, called a *filament* (fĭl′ə mənt). When you turn the light switch on, electricity begins to flow through the filament. The electricity heats up the filament until it is red hot. This red glow is the light the bulb makes.

But, of course, the incandescent bulb also makes heat. That heat energy is not used. Now there is a bulb that gives off light but not heat. It is called the Litek bulb.

The inside of the Litek bulb is painted with a special chemical. When the light switch is turned on, electrical energy passes from gas inside the bulb to the chemical paint.

The paint begins to glow, giving off light.

It takes 500,000 barrels of oil to make the electricity needed to light homes using incandescent bulbs. The Litek bulb uses about one-fourth of the energy used by an incandescent bulb. So, as you can see, the Litek bulb may cost more, but it is worth the price.

1. The word in the story that means "glowing with heat" is
   _____.

2. Incandescent bulbs give off _____ that goes to waste.

3. What does the Litek bulb use to make light besides electricity
   and paint?
       a. gas
       b. oil
       c. heat

4. Instead of a filament, the Litek bulb uses a
       a. thin wire.
       b. chemical paint.
       c. light switch.

5. The advantage of using the Litek bulb is that it _____
   than the incandescent bulb.
       a. costs less to buy
       b. uses less energy
       c. burns more brightly

6. Under which of the following headings would you list the Litek
   bulb?
       a. A Bulb That Will Not Glow
       b. An Energy-Saving Bulb
       c. A Less-Expensive Bulb

Soap Is Something Else!

We use soap every day, so we take it for granted. But soap works in a remarkable way.

Soap is a kind of *detergent* (dĭ tûr ' jənt). Detergents are used with water to clean soiled, or dirty, surfaces. Detergents attach themselves to the dirt and remove it from the material. The dirt stays in the water until it is rinsed away.

Soap comes in many different shapes, sizes, and colors. There are bars, flakes, grains, liquids, and tablets. Some soaps have perfumes and all sorts of ingredients in them. Some of these ingredients are lettuce juice, honey, and oatmeal.

But the chief ingredients in all soaps are fats and *alkalis* (ăl′kə līz′). An alkali is a very strong substance that joins with acids to make salts. Lye is the alkali most often used in making soap.

Soap works because it makes water wetter. Soap causes the water to become droplets and to spread out. Then the water can soak the soiled material more easily. Bubbles and suds form, but they do not help in the cleaning process.

Daily washing with soap prevents dirt and body oil from clogging the skin's pores. Soap kills germs that may cause infections in sores and wounds. Soap also causes "bathtub ring" when it reacts with minerals in the water and forms lime soap, or soapcurd. Then you have to clean the bathtub to clean up the soap!

1. Something used with water to clean soiled surfaces is called a
    _____ .

2. The main ingredients in soap are fats and _____ .

3. Soap works because it
    a. makes bubbles and suds.
    b. can be used in bath water to foam soapcurd.
    c. makes water wetter, causing it to spread out.

4. When soap reacts with the minerals in water, it forms
    a. "bathtub ring," or lime soap.
    b. salts and acids.
    c. a very strong substance called lye.

5. Which of the following happens *first?*
    a. The dirt is rinsed away by water.
    b. The dirt is pulled away from the material.
    c. The detergent attaches itself to the dirt.

6. Carol falls and cuts her knee. Her friend, Lee, puts a bandage
    on the cut right away. Has Lee done the right thing?
    a. Yes. The bandage will keep the cut clean.
    b. No. The cut should have been washed first.
    c. No. Lee should have left the cut alone.

Up They Go

Hot-air balloons are not only fun; they provide scientists with important information.

In 1978, millions of people listened for the latest news about *Double Eagle II*, a hot-air balloon. The balloon's three passengers hoped to be the first persons to successfully cross the Atlantic Ocean in a wind-powered vehicle. They rode in the balloon's *gondola* (gŏn′dl ə). A gondola is a basket suspended, or hung, from a balloon.

The balloon was launched in Maine on August 11, 1978. After 137 hours and 6 minutes in the air, *Double Eagle II* touched down in France on August 17, 1978. Three joyful passengers climbed out of the gondola. Their flight had been a success!

The first hot-air balloon was flown in France in 1783. The passengers in the gondola of that balloon, however, were not people. They were a duck, a rooster, and a sheep!

A few years later, a French meteorologist, or weather scientist, found

a new use for hot-air balloons. The meteorologist sent up weather instruments in the balloon's gondola. The instruments collected information about air temperature, wind direction, and speed.

Today, balloons are important tools of meteorologists. They provide valuable information about weather conditions throughout the world.

1. The passenger section of a hot-air balloon is called the
   _____ .

2. The first hot-air balloon was launched in the year _____ .

3. The *Double Eagle II* was a _____-powered hot-air balloon.

4. Why did the *Double Eagle II* make history?
   a. It was watched by millions of people.
   b. It was equipped with special weather instruments.
   c. It successfully crossed the Atlantic with passengers.

5. Today's use of balloons by weather scientists can probably be traced back to
   a. a French meteorologist of the 1700s.
   b. the first hot-air balloon launched in France.
   c. the *Double Eagle II*, which landed in France.

6. Ballooning is also becoming a fast-growing sport. Using the scale below, how would ballooning rate in terms of adventure and personal danger?

SCALE
1 – 3 → Low
4 – 7 → Medium
8 – 10 → High

   a. 2   b. 6   c. 9

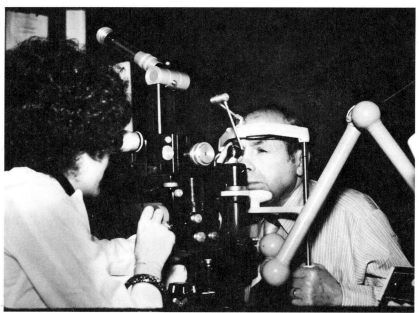

Super Light

Lasers, super-strong beams of light, are used for many purposes.

A doctor has discovered a detached *retina* (rĕt′n ə) in a patient's eye. In the past, this detached retina might have meant a loss of sight in that eye. But today, an amazing tool makes delicate eye surgery possible.

The tool is a *laser* (lā′zər), a super-strong beam of light. By carefully directing this super light beam, the doctor can *weld* (wĕld), or join, the retina to the eye again. Not only doctors, but engineers, dentists, and others are finding many uses for the laser.

The laser beam is made of the same kind of light that shines from a lamp. The light from a lamp is diffused, or spread out, over a room. Scientists have found that by shining light through certain crystals or gases, they can keep the light from spreading. At the same time, the light becomes *amplified* (ăm′plə fīd′), or stronger, as mirrors reflect it back and forth through the crystal or gas. In this way, the light is forced to move in one straight super beam—a laser beam. The word laser stands for *L*ight *A*mplification by *S*timulated *E*mission of *R*adiation. You can see why it is easier to say laser.

The super heat of the laser beam also can be used to mend and join pieces of metal and to burn away the dirt from stone buildings. Lasers are used in hospitals to sterilize instruments, stop bleeding, and mend tiny wounds in such areas as the eye or the ear.

1. A laser can be described as a _____.

2. Pieces of metal can be welded together by using laser
   a. gas.
   b. heat.
   c. crystals.

3. In this story, a doctor has used a laser beam to
   a. sterilize instruments before an operation.
   b. keep a patient from losing too much blood.
   c. save a patient's eyesight.

4. One major difference between lamplight and a laser is that lamplight
   a. is much brighter than a laser.
   b. spreads out in all directions.
   c. contains more heat than a laser.

5. The crystals or gases in this story act something like a
   a. flashlight
   b. surgeon's needle.
   c. loudspeaker.

6. Under which of the following headings would you list the laser the doctor uses?
   a. A Dangerous Weapon
   b. A Miracle Tool
   c. An Uncertain Experiment

Ball Lightning

Ball lightning is still a mystery to many scientists.

Ball lightning is lightning that looks like balls of fire in the sky. The "balls" may be as small as a pea or as large as a basketball. They fall from clouds and explode when they hit the ground. When this happens, the ground looks as if it were lit up by brilliant fireworks. Other times, the "balls" will roll slowly along the ground until they hit something in their path. Then they explode as lightning.

There is very little known about ball lightning. In fact, so far, there is no reasonable scientific explanation for this strange form of lightning. This leads some to believe that ball lightning may just be an *optical illusion*

(ŏp′tĭ kəl ĭ lōō′zhən). An optical illusion is a sight that fools the eyes. It may look real, but it is not. However, many people say they have seen ball lightning strike. So scientists have continued their study of this lightning, and they have even tried to produce it in the laboratory.

Unlike ordinary lightning, ball lightning has rarely been known to harm poeple. But it has been known to damage homes and buildings.

If you ever see ball lightning, try to observe carefully what happens. Then, write down your observations. Maybe your report will be the one that explains the mystery of ball lightning.

1. The term in the story that describes a sight that fools the eyes is an _____ .

2. The story says that ball lightning seems to appear like _____ in the sky.
   - a. peas
   - b. balls of fire
   - c. basketballs

3. Ball lightning has been known to kill many people.
   - a. True
   - b. False
   - c. The story does not say.

4. The story leads you to believe that
   - a. ball lightning does not really exist.
   - b. scientists do not know what causes ball lightning.
   - c. ball lightning will usually travel in one path.

5. When ball lightning rolls along the ground, it eventually
   - a. disappears into the ground.
   - b. explodes as lightning.
   - c. bounces back into the clouds.

6. Based on what you just read, under which heading would you list ball lightning?
   - a. The Most Dangerous Lightning
   - b. The Loudest Lightning
   - c. The Least Understood Lightning

What about Wind Power?

Wind power is one of our oldest sources of energy.

Wind-powered ships were used in Egypt 8,000 years ago. The Persians used windmills about 1,400 years ago. Some people can remember the beauty of the clipper ships that once sailed the seas. Now that fuels, such as oil, are in short supply, people are once again looking to the wind as a source of energy.

Today, wind power is being used to *generate* (jĕn'ə rāt'), or make, electrical energy. The electrical energy is used for heating and lighting homes and other buildings. Although the cost of a wind-powered generator can be high, the wind, itself, costs nothing, and the supply is endless.

However, we cannot always depend on the wind. For one thing, wind does not blow in all places at all times. Also, winds are stronger in some places than in others. Unprotected areas have the best opportunities to use wind energy. Such places include coastlines and large, flat areas, such as plains, deserts, oceans, and lakes. Wind can be slowed down by forests, mountains, and hills.

One problem with wind generators is how to keep them from breaking apart in very strong winds. A windmill generator near Denver, Colorado, for example, fell from its tower during a 144 kph windstorm. Engineers and construction workers are testing various materials and designs for strength.

1. The word in the passage that means the same as "to make" is
   _____ .

2. The wind has been used as an energy source since ancient times.
       a. True   b. False   c. The story does not say.

3. This story tells us that, as an energy source, the wind may *best* be considered as
       a. dependable.   b. old-fashioned.   c. cheap.

4. Based on what you have just read, if you wanted to use the wind to make the electricity needed to light your home, you would most probably
       a. need a back-up source for windless days.
       b. have to live in a valley or wooded area.
       c. need to live in a protected area or place.

Use the table below to answer questions 5 and 6.

AVERAGE KPH WINDS AT SOME WEATHER STATIONS IN THE UNITED STATES
(computed through 1977)

Location	Average Speed	Location	Average Speed
Bismarck, ND	16.8 kph	Detroit, MI	16.3 kph
Boston, MA	20.2 kph	Galveston, TX	17.6 kph
Buffalo, NY	19.7 kph	Key West, FL	17.9 kph
Cape Hatteras, NC	18.6 kph	Minneapolis, MN	16.8 kph
Chicago, IL	16.6 kph	Omaha, NE	18.9 kph
Cleveland, OH	17.3 kph	San Francisco, CA	16.8 kph

5. In which two cities would wind-powered generators work best?
   _____ .

6. According to the table, wind speed is *lowest* at the weather station in _____ .

107

Geothermal Power

Using the earth's heat may be one way to meet our energy needs.

The word *geothermal* (jē′ō thûr′məl) means "earth heat." Geothermal energy is formed when the earth's great heat meets water. This usually occurs in pockets of very hot rock under the earth's surface. Heat from deep inside the earth seeps up slowly into these geothermal pockets. When water from above and under the ground meets this heat, the water becomes super hot, or very, very hot.

Sometimes the super-hot water forces its way through cracks in the earth's surface. If the water flows out, hot springs are formed. But if it shoots upward with force, great streams, or *geysers* (gī′zərz), of steam and hot water are formed. Old Faithful, the geyser in Yellowstone National Park, is an example of super-hot water that has reached the earth's surface. In most places, however, the super-hot water is trapped under cap rock.

One company in California is drilling wells 2,100 to 3,000 meters deep through this solid cap rock to get to the steam below. The steam is then piped to the surface, where it is used to drive the turbine generators that make electricity. About 200 wells now supply enough steam to generate 608,000 kilowatts of electricity. This is enough electricity to meet the needs of 600,000 customers in the area.

The use of geothermal energy in the United States and other countries is still quite small. But further experiments with it could provide some answers to the world's energy problems.

1. The word *geothermal* means _____.

2. What happens when the earth's great heat meets water?
   a. Geothermal energy is formed.
   b. A hot-rock pocket is formed.
   c. Electricity is produced.

3. According to the story, geysers form when super-hot water
   a. seeps down into pockets of hot rock.
   b. shoots upward with great force.
   c. flows through cracks in the earth's surface.

4. Number the events below in the order in which they happen.
   ____ Deep wells are drilled.
   ____ Turbine generators produce electricity.
   ____ Steam is used to drive turbine generators.
   ____ Pipes carry steam to the earth's surface.

Use the diagram below to answer questions 5 and 6.

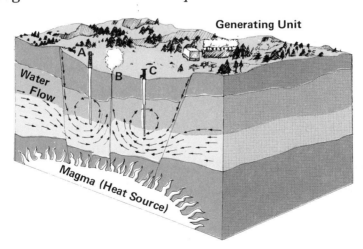

5. The part of the diagram that is labeled B is called a
   a. geyser.   b. drill rig.   c. well.

6. The heat that changes the water to steam would come from the part of the diagram that is labeled _____.

Natural Gas, A Fuel for Cars

Imagine running a car on the fuel we use for cooking.

Such a car may not be too far away. The fuel is called natural gas, or methane (meth'ān). Methane is a colorless gas. It is one of the basic building blocks of which living things are made.

Why would natural gas make such a good fuel for a car? It contains more energy than coal, oil, or gasoline. It is safer than gasoline since it is lighter than air. When it leaks, it drifts harmlessly away. When natural gas burns, it causes very little pollution. It is clean burning. And that means an engine fueled by natural gas will last longer. Natural gas is already carried easily and cheaply by pipeline to most areas. It is used to heat homes and water, and to cook food.

Cars cannot be fueled directly from the pipeline. The natural gas must be pumped into special tanks which make it more concentrated, or pressurized. It takes up more room than gasoline. So the fuel tanks in cars would have to be changed. Or drivers would have to refuel more often. Perhaps someday you will drive into a service station and say, "Fill it up with natural gas."

1. Methane, a basic part of all things, is a colorless _____.

2. When methane burns, it
   a. drifts harmlessly away.
   b. gives off oil.
   c. causes pollution.

3. According to the story, scientists have found a cheap way to
   a. carry methane to communities.
   b. separate methane from water.
   c. store methane in tanks.

4. Methane would make a cleaner fuel than gasoline.
   a. True   b. False   c. The story does not say.

5. The story suggests that if methane is used in cars, then automakers must design
   a. lighter engines.
   b. larger fuel tanks.
   c. shorter car bodies.

6. Another name for this article could be:
   a. Methane—from Cooking to Cars
   b. Uses for Natural Gas
   c. Life's Basic Building Blocks

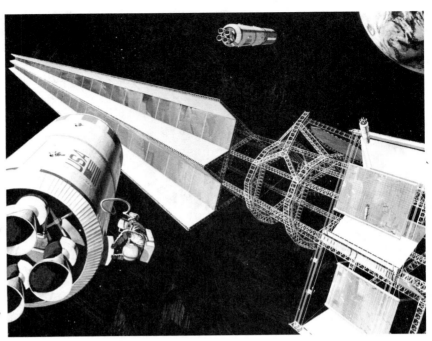

An Old Invention Gets a New Treatment

Scientists are looking at a discovery made 30 years ago.

Many scientists believe that solar energy is one of the most promising ways of providing for our future energy needs. But problems with present solar power systems have scientists looking to the past for some of the answers.

Scientists are using an invention made in the early 1950s. It is called the *photovoltaic cell* (fō'tō vŏl tā'ĭk sĕl). The photovoltaic cell, or solar cell, changes solar energy directly into electrical energy. This change takes place when sunlight hits certain materials in the cell and forms an electric current.

A photovoltaic cell measures about two centimeters square and must be made by hand. It is made of almost pure *silicon* (sĭl'ĭ kən). Silicon is an element found in abundance on Earth. But the process of purifying silicon is very expensive. Since a single photovoltaic cell generates only a little electricity, it is necessary to combine many cells and expose them to the sun. Then enough electricity can be generated to do a variety of jobs. In fact, electricity made with photovoltaic cells has powered more than 98 percent of the space vehicles placed in orbit. Also, photovoltaic cells are used in some rural, or country, areas where electric power lines and small generators are not practical.

Using photovoltaic cells to produce electricity is cleaner and more efficient than using fossil fuels or nuclear fuels. But storing electrical energy produced by the sun is a problem yet to be solved.

1. A photovoltaic cell changes _____ energy directly into electrical energy.

2. The element used to make photovoltaic cells is known as _____ .

3. Using electricity made from photovoltaic cells is both efficient and
    a. cheap.
    b. clean.
    c. common.

4. The story suggests that a single photovoltaic cell can produce
    a. enough electricity to power a spacecraft.
    b. the same amount of electricity produced by a small generator.
    c. only a very small amount of electricity.

5. Photovoltaic cells can be used in place of
    a. silicon cells.
    b. electric power lines.
    c. solar energy.

6. Which of the following areas dealing with photovoltaic electricity is still a problem?
    a. production
    b. collection
    c. storage

A Pretty Weed Packs Real Power!

The cattail plant may soon be heating homes and helping to run automobiles.

The cattail is a plant with long, thin leaves. Its stem looks more like a hot dog than a cat's tail. Cattails grow in marshes (märsh'əz). A marsh is wet land covered with shallow water. So cattails can grow where crops such as corn and wheat cannot grow.

Cattails grow so well in Minnesota that they are a problem. Each year, they have to be mowed down. Otherwise, they would cover the marshes completely, and boats could not get through. But soon cattails may be used to make a good share of the energy needed in Minnesota.

Native Americans of Minnesota have known for a long time that cattails are a good food source. They grind cattails up for flour. Now scientists are discovering other ways to use cattails. They *compress* (kəm prĕs'), or squeeze, the plants together for use as fuel in stoves and furnaces. Small pieces of compressed cattails burn for a long time. Scientists are also making alcohol from cattails. Alcohol can be mixed with gasoline to run automobiles and farm machinery.

We may someday run out of oil and coal. But a fresh crop of cattails grows every year. Cut them down and they grow right up again from their stems under the water. They live on water, sun, air, and minerals in the water. They also use up pollutants in the environment. So, in many ways, cattails are an ideal source of energy.

1. Marshland is land that is _____.

2. When you squeeze something together, you _____ it.

3. In Minnesota, the cattail plant has been a problem because it
   a. is used to make alcohol.
   b. grows over too much of the water.
   c. pollutes the environment.

4. Before we can use cattails as a fuel for automobiles, the plant must be turned into
   a. oil.
   b. gasoline.
   c. alcohol.

5. Why is it good that cattails can grow in marshes?
   a. They don't use land needed for other crops.
   b. They can be compressed easily in water.
   c. They eventually dry up the marshes.

6. Under which of the following headings would you list cattails?
   a. A Bothersome Plant
   b. A Future Energy Source
   c. An Air Pollutant

Putting Solar Energy to Work in the Classroom

A sixth-grade class helped to save energy.

A class of Colorado school children decided to build *solar collectors* (sō′lər kə lĕk′tərz) to try to heat their classroom. *Solar* means "related to the sun." Thus, a solar collector absorbs, or collects, the sun's energy. The class built four very simple solar collectors on their playground. It took a lot of work. They made airtight boxes out of wood and glass. The front side of each collector was slanted toward the sun.

The inside of each box was lined with foam to keep heat from getting out. Then, a sheet of metal was curved inside each box so that air would flow all around it. The sun would shine through the glass and onto the metal. The metal would get hot from the sun and warm the air around it inside the collectors.

But how did the class get the heat into their classroom? First, they hooked the four solar collectors together, using plastic pipe. Then, they ran pipe from a blower inside their classroom to the first collector.

The blower pushed air out of the classroom to the collectors. The air was heated and then pushed on through the boxes into another pipe. That pipe led back into the classroom. All of the pipes had to be carefully covered to keep the heat from escaping outside before it reached the classroom.

Finally, the solar heating system was ready. And it worked! For less than two hundred dollars, the class was using the sun to help heat their own room.

1. The word *solar* means _____.

2. The air in the collectors was warmed by the
     a. glass.
     b. metal.
     c. foam.

3. Why was the sheet of metal in each collector curved?
     a. to reflect the sun
     b. so heat would not escape
     c. so air could move around it

4. On the lines in front of each action, write the number that shows the order in which it happened.
     _____ Solar collectors were hooked together.
     _____ Air was heated.
     _____ A blower pushed air out of the classroom to the collectors.
     _____ A pipe was put in from the classroom to the first collector.

5. At the very end of its trip, the air was led to the
     a. collectors.
     b. metal sheets.
     c. children.

6. Which of the following would be a good location for solar collectors?
     a. a basement
     b. a cafeteria
     c. a rooftop

Rosalyn Yalow, Nobel Prize Winner

At 6:45 one morning, a phone rang in the New York office of Dr. Rosalyn Yalow. The call was from Stockholm, Sweden. The caller informed Dr. Yalow that she had won the 1977 Nobel Prize for Medicine. Dr. Yalow became the sixth woman to receive a Nobel Prize in the 77-year history of the science awards.

Dr. Yalow is Senior Medical Investigator at the Veterans' Hospital in the Bronx, New York. She grew up in New York and graduated from the city's Hunter College. In 1945, she received her doctoral degree from the University of Illinois. Then she returned to Hunter College to teach physics. Her interest in the medical uses of radioactive isotopes continued to grow.

For many years, Dr. Yalow worked with Dr. Solomon Berson, who died in 1972. Together, they developed a technique called radioimmunoassay (RIA). The method uses radioactive isotopes to measure substances in the blood and tissues of the body. These substances had been impossible to locate by other laboratory methods. RIA

is used to measure the level of insulin, a hormone that regulates the amount of sugar in the blood. RIA is also used to check blood stored in blood banks for contamination by a virus that causes hepatitis, an infection of the liver.

Dr. Yalow received the Nobel Prize for helping to develop the RIA method. Today, RIA methods are used in thousands of laboratories throughout North America and the world.

A Visit to the Exploratorium in San Francisco

"Everyone's do-it-yourself museum." That is what many people call the Exploratorium in San Francisco, California. Each year, more than 500,000 people visit the museum. The museum was built to help visitors gain a better understanding of science and technology.

The Exploratorium is a museum for touching, seeing, hearing, and exploring. Visitors can explore more than 400 exhibits.

One of the most popular exhibits in the Museum is called the Vidium. At this exhibit, a visitor sings, claps, or talks into microphones. The sounds blend together to make a design on a color television screen. Visitor can make many different sound drawings.

Another exhibit is called the Echo Tube. The Echo Tube is about 65 meters long. Inside the large tube, a visitor can hear the echo of his or her own voice. But the echo of a clap sounds like a whistle.

One of the rooms in the exhibit was built as an optical illusion. A small child standing at one end of the room looks like a giant, while an adult standing at the other end looks as small as a child.

Other exhibits deal with light, lasers, pendulums, electricity, magnets, and air pressure. Certain exhibits have become so popular that some colleges in the area use the museum to teach science.

Light and Color

Fill the spaces with the names of 16 items that relate to light, color, and shadows. The names are listed below.

5-Letter Words

light
focus
umbra
prism

6-Letter Words

camera
shadow
convex

7-Letter Words

refract
reflect
concave

8-Letter Words

spectrum
luminous

10-Letter Words

focal point
footcandle

11-Letter Words

translucent
transparent

At What Temperature Does Water Boil?

Water boils and changes to steam at 212 degrees on a Fahrenheit thermometer (212°F) and 100 degrees on a Celsius thermometer (100°C). Can you find a path from the teapot to the thermometers?

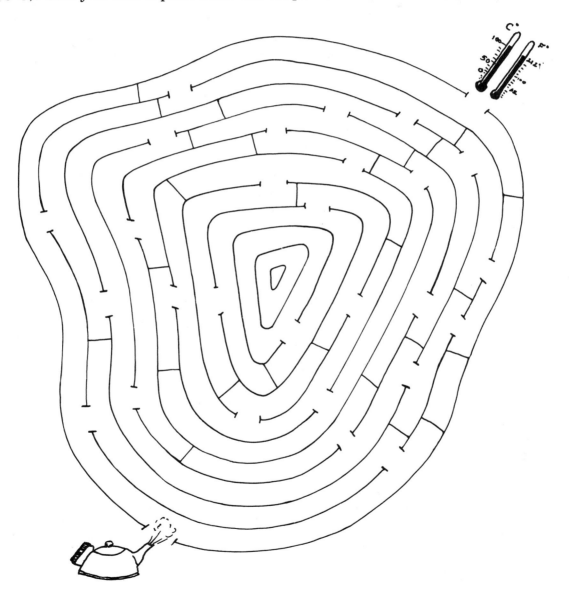

Conserving Electricity*

In most places, fossil fuels are used to produce electricity. These fuels (coal, oil, and natural gas) are limited. They must be conserved. Using less electricity helps to conserve fossil fuels.

In this science adventure, you learn to read your electric meter. You will keep a record of your family's use of electricity. You are also encouraged to try to use less electricity.

Reading an Electric Meter

A typical electric meter is shown here. It is like your water meter. The pointers on alternate dials move in opposite directions. The dials are read from left to right. Make sure to copy the numbers in the same way. When the pointer is between numbers, always read the lower number.

Electricity use is measured in units called kilowatt-hours (kwh). Do you see that the meter shown here records 13,488 kwh?

* Adapted from *Science Activities in Energy*, American Museum of Science and Energy.

Keep a record of your family's electricity use each day for a week.

	Starting Data	Day #1	Day #2	Day #3	Day #4	Day #5	Day #6	Day #7
Date								
Reading								
Electricity Used								

Conserving Electricity

Talk it over with your family. Try to get everyone to conserve electricity for one week. Some things which can be done include:

- Use all electrical appliances less. That means TVs, hair dryers, stoves, heaters, air conditioners, and lights.

- Lower the setting on your electric hot-water heater to 110°F. You might also use less hot water.

Keep a record of your family's electricity use during "conservation week."

	Starting Data	Day #1	Day #2	Day #3	Day #4	Day #5	Day #6	Day #7
Date								
Reading								
Electricity Used								

By really trying, how much electricity did your family save in a week? _____ kwh. Call your electric company. How much do they charge per kilowatt-hour of electricity used? _____. What if you conserved this much electricity every week? How much money would your family save in a year? $_____

Investigating Wind and Electricity*

It has been determined that electricity can be produced from wind. Any wind over eight miles per hour will do. Use the Beaufort Wind Scale. Check how fast the wind is blowing around your school.

Keep a record of the wind speeds at different times during the day.

When do the fastest winds usually occur?

Are the winds in your area steady or gusty?

Based on your observations, could wind be used to produce electricity in your area?

OBSERVATIONS AND DISCUSSION: _____

_____

_____

BEAUFORT WIND SCALE

Beaufort number	Description* * mph = miles per hour	Observation	
0	calm (0–1 mph)	smoke rises vertically	
1	light air (2–3 mph)	smoke drifts slowly	
2	slight breeze (4–7 mph)	leaves rustle; wind vane moves	
3	gentle breeze (8–12 mph)	twigs move; flags extended	

* Adapted from *Science Activities in Energy,* American Museum of Science and Energy.

Beaufort number	Description* * mph = miles per hour	Observation	
4	moderate breeze (13–18 mph)	branches move; dust and paper rise	
5	fresh breeze (19–24 mph)	small trees sway	
6	strong breeze (25–31 mph)	large branches sway; wires whistle	
7	moderate gale (32–38 mph)	trees in motion; walking difficult	
8	fresh gale (39–46 mph)	twigs break off trees	
9	strong gale (47–54 mph)	branches break; roofs damaged	
10	whole gale (55–63 mph)	trees snap; damage evident	
11	storm (64–72 mph)	widespread damage	
12	hurricane (73–82 mph)	extreme damage	

Where would you put a wind generator on your school ground? (Clue: Where is the windiest spot?)

What were the fastest winds measured on your school ground during the week?

CAREERS IN SCIENCE

Shelter is a basic human need. A few thousand years ago, when people needed a place to live, they built it out of whatever they could find that would protect them from the weather. To them, shelter was nothing fancy, but it served their needs.

Then people became civilized. Their needs changed, and they wanted bigger and fancier buildings. People needed more knowledge to build these fancy buildings. Builders became specialized. Today, construction is a major industry. Everywhere you look, houses, office buildings, restaurants, and shopping centers are under construction, and a lot of people are involved.

Architects design buildings. They have to know how to get the best use out of a space. They have to understand building materials, soil composition, drainage, and weather patterns or climate.

Drafters work from the architect's designs and make the plans that are actually used to construct the building. They need to know what materials are strong and how they will last. They also need to know how much these materials will cost.

Surveyors give the needed information about the building site. They determine the boundaries, or sides, of the property. They also decide exactly where the building is to be put up on the building lot.

As you can see, construction involves a number of people already. And we have not even started the building yet!

Here is a list of construction job skills and some careers in construction. Can you match them up correctly?

_____ A. pipefitter
_____ B. high ironworker
_____ C. carpenter
_____ D. welder
_____ E. electrician

1. Has a good sense of balance and no fear of heights.
2. Understands metals and their composition and can join two different pieces of metal together.
3. Puts in all the wires and electrical lights and equipment.
4. Knows about bending, threading, and cutting pipes.
5. Knows about wood and how to cut it and fit it together.

I want to give a party for all the people involved in building our house.

Then you had better rent a stadium!

Could you get all the people involved in building the place where you live to fit into it? Make a list. Don't forget the people who made the furniture, the stoves, the furnaces, electrical wires, plumbing, and the like.

A Construction Project

Design something to build: a box, a bookshelf, a picnic table (or a spaceship, if you like). Pick the construction materials (wood, metal, concrete, etc.). Try to figure out how much your project would cost. (Estimate the cost.) Remember: some materials, such as wood, come in standard sizes but are charged by some other measurement. (You buy lumber by the "board foot.") You do not have to build your project.

Simply estimate the cost. The cost may surprise you.
Find the hourly wages where you live for the following occupations:
roofer
plumber
framing carpenter
painter
mason

Which occupations work outdoors? Which work indoors? Which of the occupations have the best salary for the entire year?

Here is a different kind of construction occupation. This person's job begins when everyone else's job is completed. And it is an outdoor job. The job could be considered a "finishing touch." You would notice the person's job outside the building.

This person has studied engineering, ecology, horticulture (the growing of plants), and drafting. This person works as a _____ _____. (Unscramble the clue: sclepadan theracict)

Here is a new word to impress your friends with: *theodolite* (thē ŏd′ə līt′). It is a word that is used in a construction occupation. Look it up in a dictionary and see what occupation uses a theodolite and what is done with it.

The world seems to be shrinking. And we are causing it to shrink. The first trip around the world took place less than five hundred years ago. It took almost three years for Magellan's ships to sail around the world. But we can go anywhere in the world now in a matter of hours. We can transport people, food, construction materials, machines, and medical supplies by air, land, or sea. The earth has become smaller because of the shorter amount of time it now takes to travel on it. Our way of life depends on this fast travel or transportation.

- **Aircraft designers** planned the aircraft.
- **Aircraft engineers** determined the best and safest metals and other materials to use in building the aircraft. Other engineers developed aircraft fuels, electronic equipment, safety equipment, and tools for repairing the aircraft.

- **Airline pilots** are highly trained and skilled people who know how to fly their aircraft and to operate all of its complicated equipment. Every flight today, though, depends upon hundreds of other science careers.
- **Meteorologists** (weather experts) help the pilots plan safe routes and tell them what weather to expect. They also warn pilots of areas where it is not safe to fly. Meteorologists are also important to transportation on land and sea.

Ocean transportation careers also depend on science.

- **Oceanographers** have mapped the oceans, the usual or prevailing winds, and the movement of ocean currents. All of this has helped to make ocean shipping safer and faster.

Science careers have also greatly helped land transportation.

- **Chemists** have developed safer tires and oils which also provide more protection and last longer.

How many items in your home had to be brought there by some kind of transportation? How many items came from your local area? How many came from long distances away? Can you name some that came by air? by sea? by rail? in a truck? Make a list, like the one below, for a number of items in your home. Use this code key to show how the items got to you.

KEY			
air ○○○		rail ——————	
sea ⌣⌣⌣⌣		highway _ _ _	

LOCALLY PRODUCED		U.S. PRODUCED		PRODUCED IN ANOTHER COUNTRY	
ITEM	CODE	ITEM	CODE	ITEM	CODE

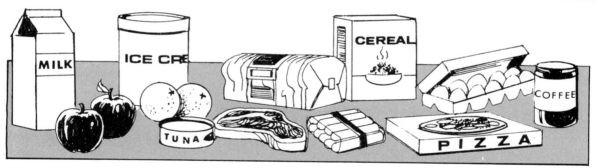

Here are some foods that you can find in your local supermarket. Can you list some of the transportation and construction careers using science which helped make it possible for you to buy these foods?

Here are some helpful hints. For each food, ask yourself:

• Was this food processed in any way?
• How did the food get to the supermarket?
• How is this food stored?
• What keeps this food from spoiling?

A Transportation Crossword Puzzle

Across

2. Finding your way at sea or in the air is called _____.
5. Engines need _____.
6. Small, strong boat that helps other ships to dock.
7. Type of transportation which is human-powered.
9. Most large present-day aircraft are ____-powered.
10. The fastest modern transportation is by _____.
11. Meteorologists study _____.
14. Some people park their cars in a _____.

Down

1. Speed indicator, air and sea.
2. Abbreviation for northeast.
3. Aircraft instrument for determining how far up you are.
4. A typical means for transporting goods is a _____.
8. Ships travel on the _____.
12. Some people use the _____ every day.
13. Another aid to finding your way is a _____.

Word List: air   altimeter   fuel garage   highway   jet   knot   map navigation   NE   rickshaw   sea truck   tug   weather

The Whole Alphabet?

Sure. See if you can think up a type of transportation that begins with each letter in the alphabet.
A—airplane   B—boat   C—car
   There. We've done the hard ones for you. Good luck!

A Bonus Boggler!

Ship some special tile to your house from Milan, Italy.
   What is the best way for you to do it? (Assume that air freight is too expensive.)
   What is the most direct route to your house?
   Trace the route on a map.
Indicate the type of transportation.

WORDS TO KNOW

The following words are found in the stories throughout this book. The words are listed according to the page on which they appear.

Many of the science books and magazines that you use contain some or all of these words. So it is important that you know the meaning of each word as it is used in science. This will make it easier for you to read and understand science materials.

Use a dictionary or a glossary of science terms to find the meanings and pronunciations of those words that are not familiar to you. You may want to record this information in your own personal "word bank."

LIFE SCIENCE UNIT

p. 14
albino
astonishment
mammals
melanin
rare
salamanders

p. 16
choosy
considered
life-styles
prey
produce
species
strand
themselves
victims
whether

p. 18
active
amphibian
creatures

deflates
develop
female
humidity
imitate
kilometer
mature
produced
remarkable
series
surviving
usually

p. 20
collected
contains
female
fertilized
method
monarch butterfly
nectar
pistils
pollen
pollination
reproduce
simply
stamens
usually

p. 22
chemicals
considered
frequently
humidity
scenery
support
tendrils
usually

p. 24
claim
created
exists
generation
gorilla
imaginary
kilograms
legends
meters
monster
ridges
soles

p. 26
banning
include
kilograms
poachers

increase
naturally
tusks
worldwide

p. 28
aluminum
cleanup
ecology
environment
materials
recycling
resources
sprouting

p. 30
annoying
examined
inhalation
palate
snoring
tissue
uvula
vibrate

p. 32
constricting
meters
poisonous
prey

seriously
usually
victim

p. 34
female
life cycle
mate
nymph
series
stray
usually

p. 36
endangered
female
identify
locate
series
signal
temperature
tigress

p. 38
coil
diary

layer
nautilus
theory
usually

p. 40
antifreeze
basic
chemical
circulates
crystals
microscope
oxygen
patient's
surgery

p. 42
arthritis
aspirin

chemicals
cinchona
disease
effective
foxglove
ignore
ingredient
joints
liquids
malaria
native
quinine
recommended
remedy
research
synthetic
yam

p. 44
actually
breeding grounds
females
identifying
mammal
mate
produce
research
species
unusual
usually

p. 46
calories
desserts
energy
fructose
intake
labels
minerals
natural
percent
products
protein
refined

sucrose
supplies
unit
useless
usually

p. 48
backbone
create
disease
encouraging
illness
nationwide
operation
posture
pressure
required
scoliosis
serious
severe
spine
surgery
therefore

EARTH-SPACE SCIENCE UNIT

p. 60
atmosphere
citrus
coastline
conditions
data
detect
environmental
error
include
marshes
monitor

overcast
polar-orbiting
satellites
scientists
shrimp
specialists
stationary
threatened

p. 62
century
corona
darkened
eclipse
energy
event
filters
nighttime
solar
whimpered

p. 64
attracted
conduct
current
discharge
energy
information
lightning
meteorologists
object
occurs
opposite
release
satellites
struck
usually

p. 66
fossils
paleontologists
preserved
probably
scent

p. 68
adapting
ancient
archaeology
located
methods
objects
plastic
recover
research
usually

p. 70
calm
jagged
mass
pressure
shifting
support
usually

p. 72
generators
habitat
irrigating
potable
powerhouses
produces
provide
rainfall
recreation
turbines
waterfowl
waterway

p. 74
erupted
evidence
explosion
information
material
meteorite
objects
origin
originated

produced
similar
suggested
tektites
theories

p. 76
actually
ancient
bog
common
evidence
extinct
fossils
hemlock
larch
mastodon
meters
peat
spruce
unusually

p. 78
astronomer
comet
explosion
kilometers
main
revolving

p. 80
alert
avoid
especially
glacier
layer
monitor
polar
pressure

p. 82
collected
colony
energy
engineers

future
gravity
necessities
position
providing
relation
solar
steady
weightless

PHYSICAL SCIENCE UNIT

p. 94
bacteria
energy
germs
liquid
manure
methane
natural
pipeline
special
substances
supplying

p. 96
chemical
energy
filament
incandescent

p. 98
alkalis
clogging
detergent
droplets
germs

infections
liquids
material
minerals
pores
process
reacts
rinsed
substances

p. 100
collected
gondola
information
instruments
launched
meteorologist
successfully
vehicle

p. 102
amplified
crystals
delicate
detached
diffused
laser
patient's
retina
sterilize
surgery
weld

p. 104
brilliant
explanation
explode
illusion
laboratory
observe
optical
produce
reasonable

PROGRESS CHART FOR LIFE SCIENCE UNIT

Questions Page	Comprehension Question Numbers				Total Number Correct per Story
	Science Vocabulary	Literal	Interpretive	Applied	
15	1	2,3	4,5	6	
17	1	2,3	4,5	6	
19	1	2,3	4,5,6		
21	1,2	3	4,5	6	
23	1	2,3	4,5	6	
25	1	2,3	4,5	6	
27	1	2,3	4,5,6		
29	1	2,3	4,5	6	
31	1	2,3	4,5,6		
33	1	2,3	4,5	6	
35	1	2	3,4,5,6		
37	1,2	3	4,5,6		
39	1	2	3,4,5	6	
41	1	2,3	4,5	6	
43	1	2,3	4,5	6	
45	1	2,3	4,5	6	
47	1	2,3	4,5	6	
49	1	2,3	4,5,6		
Total Correct per Question Type					

KEEPING A RECORD OF YOUR PROGRESS

The Progress Charts on these pages are for use with the questions that follow the stories in the Life Science, Earth-Space Science, and Physical Science Units. Keeping a record of your progress will help you to see how well you are doing and where you need to improve. Use the charts in the following way:

After you have checked your answers, look at the first column, headed "Questions Page." Read down the column until you find the row with the page number of the questions you have completed. Put an X through the number of each question in the row that you answered correctly. Add the number of correct answers, and write your total score in the last column in that row.

After you have done the questions for several stories, check to see which questions you answered correctly. Which ones were incorrect? Is there a pattern? For example, you may find that you have answered most of the literal comprehension questions correctly but that you are having difficulty answering the applied comprehension questions. If so, then this is an area in which you need help.

When you have completed all the stories in a unit, write the total number of correct answers at the bottom of each column.

PROGRESS CHART FOR EARTH-SPACE SCIENCE UNIT

Questions Page	Comprehension Question Numbers				Total Number Correct per Story
	Science Vocabulary	Literal	Interpretive	Applied	
61	1	2,3	4,5	6	
63	1	2,3	4,5	6	
65	1	2,3	4,5,6		
67	1	2,3	4,5	6	
69	1	2,3	4,5	6	
71	1	2,3	4,5	6	
73	1	2,3	4,5	6	
75	1	2,3	4	5,6	
77	1	2,3	4,5,6		
79	1	2	3,4	5,6	
81	1	2,3	4,5	6	
83	1	2	3,4,5	6	
Total Correct per Question Type					

PROGRESS CHART FOR PHYSICAL SCIENCE UNIT

Questions Page	Comprehension Question Numbers				Total Number Correct per Story
	Science Vocabulary	Literal	Interpretive	Applied	
95	1,2	3	4,5	6	
97	1	2	3,4,5	6	
99	1	2,3	4,5	6	
101	1	2,3	4,5	6	
103	1	2,3	4,5	6	
105	1	2,3	4,5	6	
107	1	2	3,4	5,6	
109	1	2,3	4	5,6	
111	1	2,3	4	5,6	
113	1	2,3	4,5	6	
115	1,2	3	4,5	6	
117	1	2,3	4,5	6	
Total Correct per Question Type					

BIBLIOGRAPHY

Books on Life Science

Books on Life Science

Amon, Aline. *Roadrunners and Other Cuckoos*. New York: Atheneum, 1978.

Borland, Hal. *The Golden Circle: A Book of Months*. New York: Crowell, 1977.

Bright, Michael. *Pollution & Wildlife*, Survival Series. New York: Gloucester Press, 1987.

Cochrane, Jennifer. *Land Energy*, Project Ecology Series. New York: Bookwright Press, 1987.

Cooper, Gale. *Inside Animals*. Boston: Atlantic: Little, Brown, 1978.

Epstein, Sam and Beryl. *Dr. Beaumont and the Man with the Hole in His Stomach*. illustrated by Joseph Scrofani. New York: Coward, 1978.

Fegely, Thomas D. *The World of Fresh Water Fish*. New York: Dodd, Mead, 1978.

Ford, Barbara. *Animals That Use Tools*. illustrated by Janet P. D'Amato. New York: Messner, 1978.

Foster, Laura Louise. *Keeping the Plants You Pick*. New York: Crowell, 1970.

Hess, Lilo. *Secrets in the Meadow*. New York: Scribners, 1980.

Hussey, Lois J. and Catherine Pessino. *Collecting for the City Naturalist*. illustrated by Barbara Neill. New York: Crowell, 1975.

Hutchins, Ross E. *Nature Invented It First*. New York: Dodd, Mead, 1980.

Leen, Nina. *Snakes*. New York: Holt, 1978.

Limburg, Peter. *What's in the Name of Wild Animals*. illustrated by Murray Tinkelman. New York: Coward, 1977.

McLaughlin, Molly. *Earthworms, Dirt, & Rotten Leaves: An Exploration in Ecology*. New York: Atheneum, 1986.

Malatesta, Anne and Ronald Friedland. *The White Kikuyu: Louis S. B. Leakey*, New York: McGraw-Hill, 1978.

Pringle, Laurence. *Listen to the Crows*. New York: Crowell, 1976.

Soucie, Anita Holmes. *Plant Fun: Ten Easy Plants to Grow Indoors*. New York: Four Winds Press, 1974.

Strong, Arline. *Veterinarian, Doctor for Your Pet*. New York: Atheneum, 1977.

Wise, William. *Animal Rescue*. illustrated by Heidi Palmer. New York: G. P. Putnam's Sons, 1978.

Books on Earth-Space Science

Ames, Gerald and Rose Wyler. *The Story of the Ice Age*. illustrated by Thomas Voter. New York: Harper, 1956.

Ault, Phil. *These are the Great Lakes*. New York: Dodd, Mead, 1972.

Berger, Melvin. *The National Weather Service*. New York: John Day, 1971.

Blair, Carvel. *Exploring the Sea: Oceanography Today*. New York: Random House, 1986.

Branley, Franklyn M. *Sunshine Makes the Seasons* rev. ed. New York: Crowell, 1986.

Brindze, Ruth. *Hurricanes: Monster Storms from the Sea*. New York: Atheneum, 1973.

Gallob, Edwards. *City Rocks, City Blocks, and the Moon*. New York: Charles Scribner's Sons, 1973.

Laycock, George. *Beyond the Arctic Circle*. New York: Four Winds Press, 1978.

_____. *Caves*. illustrated by DeVere E. Burt. New York: Four Winds Press, 1976.

Pollard, Michael. *Air, Water, Weather*. New York, Facts on File, 1987.

Schlein, Miriam. *On the Track of the Mystery Animal*. New York: Four Winds Press, 1979.

Schultz, Gwen. *Icebergs and Their Voyages*. New York: Morrow, 1975.

Simon, Seymour. *Danger from Below—Earthquakes: Past, Present, and Future*. New York: Four Winds Press, 1979.

Smith, Norman F. *The Atmosphere*. Austin, Texas: Steck-Vaughan, 1975.

Stoff, Joshua. *The Voyage of the Ruslan: The First Manned Exploration of Mars*. New York: Atheneum, 1986.

Weiss, Malcolm E. *Storms—From the Inside Out*. New York: Messner, 1973.

Books on Physical Science

Aylesworth, Thomas G. *Science at the Ballgame*. New York: Walker, 1977.

Bendick, Jeanne. *Why Things Work: A Book About Energy*. New York: Parents' Magazine Press, 1972.

Berger, Melvin. *Atoms, Molecules, & Quarks*. New York: Putnam, 1986.

Branley, Franklyn M. *The End of the World*. New York: Crowell, 1974.

_____. *Energy for the Twenty-First Century*. New York: Crowell, 1975.

_____. *Color: From Rainbow to Lasers*. illustrated by Henry Roth. New York: Crowell, 1978.

Chase, Sarah B. *Moving to Win: The Physics of Sports*. New York: Messner, 1977.

Collins, Michael. *Energy for the Twenty-First Century*. New York: Crowell, 1975.

Cross, Wilbur. *Solar Energy*, Science & Technology Series. Chicago: Childrens Press, 1984.

Gallant, Roy A. *Fires in the Sky—The Birth and Death of Stars*. New York: Four Winds Press, 1979.

Halacy, Dan. *Nuclear Energy*. New York: Watts, 1984.

Landt, Dennis. *Catch the Wind: A Book of Windmills and Windpower*. New York: Four Winds Press, 1976.

Lewis, Bruce. *Meet the Computer*. illustrated by Leonard Kessler. New York: Dodd, Mead, 1977.

Veglahn, Nancy. *The Mysterious Rays: Marie Curie's World*. illustrated by Victor Juhasz. New York: Coward, 1977.

Wilson, Mike and Robin Scagell. *Jet Journal*. New York: Viking, 1978.

METRIC TABLE

This table tells you how to change customary
units of measure to metric units of measure.
The answers you get will not be exact.

LENGTH

Symbol	When You Know	Multiply by	To Find	Symbol
in	inches	2.5	centimeters	cm
ft	feet	30	centimeters	cm
yd	yards	0.9	meters	m
mi	miles	1.6	kilometers	km

AREA

Symbol	When You Know	Multiply by	To Find	Symbol
in^2	square inches	6.5	square centimeters	cm^2
ft^2	square feet	0.09	square meters	m^2
yd^2	square yards	0.8	square meters	m^2
mi^2	square miles	2.6	square kilometers	km^2
	acres	0.4	hectares	ha

MASS (weight)

Symbol	When You Know	Multiply by	To Find	Symbol
oz	ounces	28	grams	g
lb	pounds	0.45	kilograms	kg
	short tons (2000 lb)	0.9	tonnes	t

VOLUME

Symbol	When You Know	Multiply by	To Find	Symbol
tsp	teaspoons	5	milliliters	mL
Tbsp	tablespoons	15	milliliters	mL
fl oz	fluid ounces	30	milliliters	mL
c	cups	0.24	liters	L
pt	pints	0.47	liters	L
qt	quarts	0.95	liters	L
gal	gallons	3.8	liters	L
ft^3	cubic feet	0.03	cubic meters	m^3
yd^3	cubic yards	0.76	cubic meters	m^3

TEMPERATURE (exact)

Symbol	When You Know	Multiply by	To Find	Symbol
°F	Fahrenheit temperature	5/9 (after sub-tracting 32)	Celsius temperature	°C

METRIC TABLE

This table tells you how to change metric
units of measure to customary units of measure.
The answers you get will not be exact.

LENGTH

Symbol	When You Know	Multiply by	To Find	Symbol
mm	millimeters	0.04	inches	in
cm	centimeters	0.4	inches	in
m	meters	3.3	feet	ft
m	meters	1.1	yards	yd
km	kilometers	0.6	miles	mi

AREA

Symbol	When You Know	Multiply by	To Find	Symbol
cm^2	square centimeters	0.16	square inches	in^2
m^2	square meters	1.2	square yards	yd^2
km^2	square kilometers	0.4	square miles	mi^2
ha	hectares (10,000 m^2)	2.5	acres	

MASS (weight)

Symbol	When You Know	Multiply by	To Find	Symbol
g	grams	0.035	ounces	oz
kg	kilograms	2.2	pounds	lb
t	tonnes (1000 kg)	1.1	short tons	

VOLUME

Symbol	When You Know	Multiply by	To Find	Symbol
mL	milliliters	0.03	fluid ounces	fl oz
L	liters	2.1	pints	pt
L	liters	1.06	quarts	qt
L	liters	0.26	gallons	gal
m^3	cubic meters	35	cubic feet	ft^3
m^3	cubic meters	1.3	cubic yards	yd^3

TEMPERATURE (exact)

Symbol	When You Know	Multiply by	To Find	Symbol
°C	Celsius temperature	9/5 (then add 32)	Fahrenheit temperature	°F